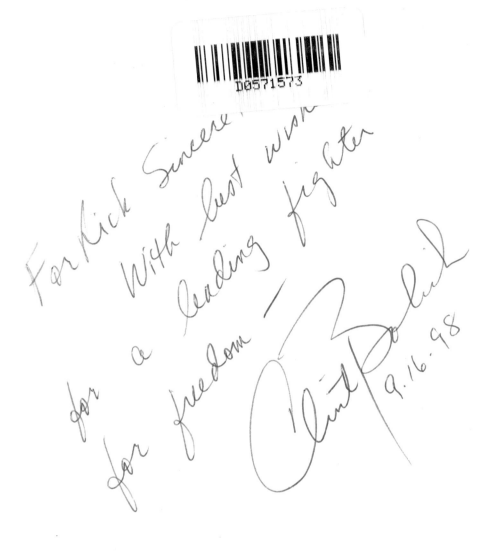

For Rick Sincere
With best wish
for a leading fighter
for freedom

9.16.98

Transformation

Transformation

The Promise and Politics of Empowerment

Clint Bolick

ICS PRESS

INSTITUTE FOR CONTEMPORARY STUDIES

Oakland, California

This book is a publication of the Institute for Contemporary Studies, a nonprofit, non-partisan public policy research organization. The analyses, conclusions, and opinions expressed in ICS Press publications are those of the authors and not necessarily those of the Institute or of its officers, its directors, or others associated with, or funding, its work.

Inquiries, book orders, and catalog requests should be addressed to ICS Press, Latham Square, 1611 Telegraph Avenue, Suite 902, Oakland, CA 94612. Tel. (510) 238-5010; Fax (510) 238-8440; Internet www.icspress.com. For book orders and catalog requests, call toll-free in the United States: (800) 326-0263.

Cover and interior design by Rohani Design, Edmonds, WA. Book set in Garamond by Rohani Design and printed and bound by R. R. Donnelly & Sons.

0 9 8 7 6 5 4 3 2 1

Library of Congress Cataloging-in-Publication Data

Bolick, Clint.
    Transformation : the promise and politics of empowerment / Clint Bolick.
        p. cm.
    Includes bibliographical references and index.
    ISBN 1-55815-506-6
    1. United States—Social policy—1993– 2. United States—Politics and government—1993– 3. Equality—United States. 4. Free enterprise—United States. I. Title
    HN65.B64   1998
    361.6'1'0973—dc21

                                                                    98–15506
                                                                        CIP

CONTENTS

A NOTE FROM
THE PUBLISHER

Inspiration is often found where common people do uncommon things: transformations can come from the most surprising places. America is being transformed not from the top down, but from the bottom up. The real changes are being made not by the elite universities, but by individuals and communities who are demanding opportunity. How *American* these processes of transformation are!

Most of our national leaders and elite universities have opposed giving real choices and real opportunity to all citizens. As you read this book, you will glimpse the outlines of a David and Goliath story. Parents who simply want a choice of where their children go to school must fight both school administrators and teachers unions for that right. Government housing project tenants who wish to create cooperatives in order to have a stake in their communities must fight housing bureaucrats, labor unions, and greedy contractors who do not want their spoils system disturbed.

So, the reader may ask, what is a middle-class lawyer of libertarian-conservative leanings doing in common cause with communities perceived to be liberal and part of the welfare establishment? Quite simply, the old categories mean very little when it comes to transformations.

Having worked in housing projects, I share many experiences with Clint Bolick. Working with communities to build their capacities to govern their own lives is truly a revelation of the strength of the human spirit. One finds individuals and communities striving side by side to build morally based efforts that define opportunity as something practical and something spiritual. Reflecting and choosing are the basis of economic opportunity and the foundation of community.

We are publishing this book in hopes that you, the reader, not only will find the stories told here compelling and uplifting, but also will join a community of common cause to allow individuals and communities to take control of their lives. It is through this vital process that America will be reborn.

— Robert B. Hawkins, Jr., President
Institute for Contemporary Studies

ACKNOWLEDGMENTS

Within the sometimes tedious writing and publishing process, this is the part I enjoy the most: expressing appreciation to friends and colleagues who in ways both concrete and intangible helped produce the book.

First and foremost, I thank my publisher, the Institute for Contemporary Studies, which has distinguished itself as one of the nation's premier empowerment think tanks. As we head into the millennium, we need fresh thinking that challenges conventional wisdom, which is ICS's trademark. Special thanks to Robert Hawkins, Perenna Fleming, and Melissa Stein for making this book possible.

My research assistant, Sabrina Sandusky, brought to this project enormous energy and enthusiasm, curiosity and compassion. Sabrina's research was thorough and resourceful and her insights generous and valuable. She is pursuing a Master of Social Work degree at Tulane

University, and her intelligence, common sense, and good will bode for a boundless future. I hope this is only our first collaboration among many. Thanks also to Chip Mellor, who read and commented on parts of the manuscript; to Gretchen Embrey, Scott Bullock, John Frantz, Kristen Webb, and David Dratch for help with research and citations; and to John Keppler and John Kramer for support on marketing and publicity.

Some of the ideas discussed here were fleshed out during a retreat in September 1997 hosted by Ellis Alden at Alden Vineyards in Geyserville, California. Those invigorating surroundings formed the backdrop for a spirited exchange of ideas among a remarkable assemblage that included Stephan and Abigail Thernstrom, Lisa Graham Keegan, Douglas Besharov, John Fund, David Tell, Terry Moe, Howard Husock, Linda Chavez, and Chip Mellor. I am grateful for the benefits of their thinking and for the support and friendship of Ellis Alden.

I am very lucky to have the opportunity to deal on a daily basis with many of the issues discussed in this book in my career as litigation director at the Institute for Justice. Our clients are the source of constant inspiration, and I applaud them for their courage and commitment and thank them for the honor of representing them. As for my colleagues at the Institute for Justice, my appreciation for their friendship, talent, and hard work goes beyond words.

I especially want to acknowledge vast accumulated debts to three individuals who are pillars of the empowerment movement and have aided greatly my own understanding and efforts in this area: Robert Woodson, Michael Joyce, and John Fund.

To Bob Woodson, founder and president of the National Center for Neighborhood Enterprise in Washington, the empowerment movement owes much of its vision and success. For two decades, Bob has redefined the civil rights struggle. He's a silver-tongued orator but an even more prodigious doer, and certainly has done more on a national scale to help poor people help themselves than any other person. Shortly after I moved to Washington as a young lawyer, Bob took me under his wing, and he hasn't stopped teaching or inspiring me since. Early in my career, I despaired when my first economic liberty client, Ego Brown, was having his utilities cut off in the middle of winter. Bob knew instantly what to do: he hosted a "rent party." The image of a group of white conservatives digging into their pockets to help Ego Brown is one I'll never forget. Nearly a decade later, Ego is a flourishing entrepreneur. Bob has taught me the necessity of activism, of listening, and of celebrating. I shall cherish our friendship always.

Michael Joyce of the Lynde and Harry Bradley Foundation in Milwaukee is one of the great visionaries of the philanthropic community. Without Mike and his colleagues, the school choice movement may never have gotten off the ground. Mike's emphasis on what he calls "silver-bullet" issues—battles like school choice that hold potential to slay the regulatory welfare state and give people greater power over their lives—has given sage direction to soldiers in the field. I'll never forget that it was Mike Joyce who provided seed funding when I hung out a shingle as a public interest lawyer in a basement office in 1988. His vision, courage, and strategic philanthropy have helped fuel many of the empowerment movement's seminal triumphs.

I have been friends with John Fund since he was a journalism student at Sacramento State University and I was a law student at the University of California at Davis. Working within the stable of talented editorial writers at the *Wall Street Journal*, John has become one of the most strategic and influential libertarian journalists in America. His relentless attacks on the education establishment for blocking the schoolhouse doors to low-income children, and on reactionary politicians and unions for erecting barriers to economic competition, have greatly aided political and litigation efforts to promote school choice and economic liberty. Many of his editorials are unsigned so he doesn't always reap due credit, but his work always bears the John Fund imprint: insightful, principled, and tenacious.

To all, my heartfelt thanks. You're the best.

INTRODUCTION

The Challenge of Empowerment

We have the power to begin the world over again.

—Thomas Paine[1]

For the past seven years, I've lived a dream come true as litigation director at the Institute for Justice in Washington, D.C. I wouldn't trade jobs with any other lawyer: my colleagues and I get to choose our cases and clients, we don't charge for our representation, and the people we sue are usually bureaucrats. It's the most gratifying way possible to make a living as a lawyer.

But it's the people we represent who make it most amazing. They're a diverse lot, spanning the ethnic, religious, and political gamuts. They all share certain qualities: they're honest, hardworking people who ask for nothing except the chance to control their own lives, but who are prevented from so doing by those who hold the reins of government power. They're people like Taalib-din Uqdah and Pamela Ferrell, trying to operate a hair-braiding business without having to satisfy the absurd dictates of cosmetology licensing officials; Pilar Gonzalez, trying to secure for her children a decent education in a safe and nurturing school; Vera Coking, trying to protect her home against confiscation by local officials who want to turn it over to Donald Trump so he can build a parking lot for his limousines; and Scott and Lou Ann Mullen, who wanted to adopt the little boy they raised from infancy but were told they couldn't because he is black and they aren't.

I like to think of myself as an articulate advocate, particularly when I care strongly about something; but I must be the only lawyer in America who can't outtalk *any* of my clients. I listen with awe as they eloquently distill the essential insights of life it took me decades to grasp. And I think to myself: these people should be masters of their own destinies—not me, not the state, some not paternalistic inter-meddler. It's tragic that in the first nation on earth grounded in the idea of individual sovereignty, people need lawyers in order to take on the legal barriers that prevent them from controlling their destinies. My purpose in writing this book is to persuade people we need to take down the barriers—particularly for those who face the toughest obstacles, yet possess the fewest resources. That's what empowerment is all about.

In the popular contemporary political lexicon, empowerment is a ubiquitous yet amorphous buzzword, an often empty vessel carrying widely different connotations depending upon who pilots it—whether Jesse Jackson on the left or Newt Gingrich on the right. Yet no better concept exists to guide efforts in the new millennium to bridge the widening chasm between the underclass and mainstream Americans.

For decades, Americans have looked to government to find solutions to help the inner-city poor. Despite the proliferation of wealth redistribu-tion and social engineering schemes, problems of inner-city poverty and despair have worsened. It seems the only solution policy makers have not explored seriously is giving power to the people themselves.

Except to the nation's intellectual and policy elite, the solutions to poverty have never been much of a mystery. They are the same mecha-nisms that have fueled countless generations of Americans to upward social and economic mobility: education and enterprise. The civil rights revolution was supposed to open those opportunities to people who had been denied them. Instead it replaced those traditional methods with welfare entitlements and race-based affirmative action. Just like other

countries that have experimented with redistributive government policies, we have discovered, painfully, that there exists no substitute to the
tried-and-true methods of education and hard work. The main victims
of the failed social experiments are those people who were the supposed
beneficiaries, who today are further separated from basic opportunities
than at any previous point in most of our lifetimes.

This book offers a clear-cut agenda for empowerment. Going far
beyond offering mere abstract policy prescriptions, it makes the case
for empowerment through the real stories of real people struggling to
overcome barriers to opportunity. Stories like the successful fight of
Freedom Cabs to break a fifty-year-old taxicab monopoly in Denver;
the battle of low-income parents in Milwaukee and Cleveland to
obtain decent educational opportunities for their children outside the
defective public schools; the challenging work of former addict Freddie
Garcia to turn around drug addicts through faith-based counseling;
and the efforts by ministers and community leaders to reclaim inner-
city streets from marauders and make them safe for ordinary people
again. The stories recounted and the policies proposed in this book are
neither new nor unusual—quite the contrary, they are classic examples
of what has always worked in this country. But after several decades
of failed social engineering, undoing the damage and securing basic
opportunities will take imagination, tenacity, and in some instances,
radical policy changes.

My experiences with many of the people and battles depicted in
this book represent a defining chapter in my own personal odyssey. I
started out preparing for a career as a schoolteacher, but turned to constitutional law when I realized that systemic barriers to opportunity
were preventing people from realizing their full potential. Initially I
approached my work primarily from an ideological standpoint, that of
a libertarian.[2] Over time I have become less ideological and more pragmatic, but in the process my passion for liberty has only intensified.
That is because I have discovered that not only is freedom right, but
freedom *works*. Time and again, when people are given greater power
and responsibility over their lives, they respond in a remarkable fashion.
That is not to say that freedom is a panacea—far from it—but it is a
precondition for progress, prosperity, community, and social harmony.

I have wanted to write this book for a long time. Most of my writing in recent years has related to affirmative action and civil rights.[3] Likewise, my colleagues and I at the Institute for Justice receive disproportionate media attention for our efforts to curb racial classifications. But most of our lawsuits challenge regulatory barriers to entrepreneurial and educational opportunities, and our clients exemplify the struggle for individual empowerment. I have been burning to tell their stories, for in their courageous stands for freedom they are the heirs to the great heroes of the civil rights movement. In a sense, this book, too, is about civil rights, for I consider empowerment the third and final stage of a movement that started with the movement to abolish slavery, then pressed forward to guarantee equal opportunity, and now awaits its ultimate vindication in securing fundamental individual rights for all Americans.

Previously that message has fallen mainly on deaf ears. True, over the past several years a growing number of intellectuals, activists, and political leaders have endorsed various empowerment initiatives. But until very recently, their efforts have gone largely unreported in the media, their urgent calls for systemic reform often unheeded.

Two epochal developments have combined to thrust empowerment to the forefront of policy debate. First is the demise of welfare as an entitlement. The cutoff of welfare benefits after a set period of time has forced policy makers to find ways to help poor people gain economic self-sufficiency—in a hurry—and to find alternative, nongovernmental means to deliver social services to needy people. The emphasis on work rather than welfare and on community rather than governmental support structures promises a far greater emphasis than ever before on finding ways to secure emancipation from poverty.

The second development is the assault on race-based affirmative action. The resulting decline in the number of black and Hispanic individuals attending elite academic institutions has sounded a long-overdue wake-up call about serious social problems that decades of affirmative action have allowed to go unaddressed. For too long, the cosmetic benefits of affirmative action have lulled us into thinking that such problems were being solved, when in reality they were festering and growing. Now we have no choice but to turn our attention to identifying and solving the causes of racial disparities that persist in most measures of success, from higher education to corporate boardrooms.

Liberals continue to attribute all such racial disparities to discrimination. No question exists that racism persists; in my view, it is exacerbated by policies—permeating every level of government—that classify and discriminate among people on the basis of race. But racism as the primary explanation for social pathologies and racial disparities simply doesn't cut it as the century draws to a close; and to insist otherwise is to ignore painful realities. Likewise, if racism suddenly were to disappear overnight, little would change for the most disadvantaged minority individuals. To the extent that liberals continue reflexively to explain racial disparities in terms of racism, at best they will continue to be irrelevant in solving other serious social problems and at worst an actual impediment.

Notably, groups and individuals who have not bought into the welfare and affirmative action agendas, but instead have invested in traditional avenues of upward economic mobility, education and enterprise, have prospered. Many recent black, Hispanic, and Asian immigrants, for example, have made enormous sacrifices to pursue business and educational opportunities. Their success is powerful testimony to the endurance of the American Dream: despite language barriers, nativist prejudice, and the necessity of grueling work in often dangerous conditions, many recent immigrants have moved swiftly up the economic ladder.

For millions of Americans, however, the dream is an illusion. Our nation's inner-city poor face so many obstacles to basic opportunities that many are defeated before they can try. Decades of perverse welfare incentives combined with abysmal public schools, declining job and business opportunities, eroding family and community structures, and soaring crime have created prospects that are bleak at best. They cannot control their destinies or obtain the means to do so. Eliminating barriers to self-determination is the object of empowerment.

Empowerment also holds promise for transforming the political landscape in a fundamental way. For decades, the American left has created a powerful constituency for redistributionist welfare state policies. As a result, whenever meaningful reform is proposed to give low-income people greater power over their lives, reactionary special interest groups— labor unions, government bureaucrats, and too often their allies in the civil rights establishment—can be counted on to mount tenacious opposition in the legislatures, courts, and media to preserve the status quo.

But the opportunity exists now to align the interests of an equally potent, if seemingly disparate, coalition behind the freedom philosophy. The reason is that, increasingly, the more tangible benefits for the poor are seen in policies that reduce government dependence rather than those that foster it. Moreover, unlike wealth redistribution and race-based affirmative action policies, empowerment draws upon shared values that most Americans hold dear, such as education, enterprise, family, and community. As a result, it offers promise in healing racial and economic divisions.

Concrete examples of empowerment strategies abound. Black parents and elected officials joined forces with conservatives to bring about school voucher programs in Milwaukee and Cleveland. A comprehensive empowerment bill, the American Community Renewal Act, unites Republican members of Congress with centrist Democrats and members of the Congressional Black Caucus. Members of the black clergy are calling for greater emphasis on entrepreneurship. Inner-city churches are enlisting in the community-based delivery of social services. All of those developments challenge conventional wisdom and illustrate a burgeoning emphasis on individual initiative and community renewal instead of the welfare state as the primary means of providing opportunities for the poor.

And they demonstrate that empowerment makes for strange political bedfellows. All of the participants bring assets and liabilities to the table. My fellow libertarians bring a freedom philosophy that has liberated from tyranny millions of people around the world. They have demonstrated that free enterprise is a prerequisite for political freedoms, and that free trade and technological advances empower individuals to control their destinies. But libertarians too often present a hard-edged, antiseptic image, and are sometimes seemingly more interested in proving abstract philosophical points than in demonstrating the freedom philosophy's tangible human benefits. A populist, problem-solving libertarianism could capture the hearts and minds of Americans just as it has done among freedom-loving people in other lands.

Conservatives bring a keen understanding of the social dimension underlying the condition of American cities, families, and the poor. Any proposed solution that ignores shared values and traditional social structures cannot endure. The free market alone, while essential to social and economic progress, is insufficient. Indeed, in many inner-city neighborhoods, a state of affairs exists akin to an unregulated state of nature, where the strong rule the weak. Only a renaissance of values, families, and community institutions can restore respect for human life, enterprise, and property. Yet some conservatives view the poor and inner cities as beyond redemption, and their unbridled pessimism over of the state of culture understates the endurance of the American system. Conservatives need to reclaim the image of optimism and opportunity personified by Ronald Reagan, as well as their belief in the vitality of the American Dream, if they are to appeal beyond their core supporters in the coming generations.

"New" Democrats have demonstrated in many instances the efficacy of reforming government. Whether libertarians or conservatives like it, most Americans are deeply committed to public institutions, such as public education and some sort of safety net. Rather than tilting at windmills, new Democrats have brought market-oriented reforms that have improved efficient delivery of social services. Still, their devotion to governmental institutions often inhibits true empowerment through private-sector solutions. If centrist Democrats can overcome their aversion to the market, they will find at their disposal many more tools with which to address serious social problems.

Empowerment cannot succeed without forward-looking minority leaders who are willing to challenge conventional wisdom. Men and women such as Supreme Court Justice Clarence Thomas, retired General Colin Powell, former U.S. Representative Floyd Flake, Representative J. C. Watts, former Virginia Governor L. Douglas Wilder, Wisconsin State Representative Annette Polly Williams, Cleveland City Councilwoman Fannie Lewis, University of California regent Ward Connerly, National Urban League president John Jacob, and National Center for Neighborhood Enterprise president Robert L. Woodson, Sr.—a list that demonstrates remarkable diversity—have all questioned prevailing orthodoxy and carried the empowerment banner. But too few minority politicians—and even fewer establishment civil rights groups—are willing to break ranks with their powerful allies in the labor unions, government bureaucracies, and the left wing of the Democratic Party. Floyd Flake, who left Congress to return to the ministry and community activism, remarks that "[w]e're still acting like it's 1967 when it's now 1997."[4] As long as politicians and organizations supposedly committed to minority progress continue to support entitlements and oppose or give lip service to empowerment, the possibilities are limited.

Among the contributors to the empowerment agenda, the intellectual foment among libertarians and conservatives is most vibrant. Some have commented that the gulf between them seems unbridgeable: libertarians are determined to reduce the size and scope of government, while conservatives want to wield the state for their own moralistic ends. Yet compare the leading political commentators on both sides, and common themes emerge. Pointing out that communism is all but dead and that Bill Clinton has adopted large parts of the Republican agenda, libertarians Virginia L. Postrel and James K. Glassman, writing in the *Wall Street Journal*, remark that "conservative pessimism seems strange."[5] They observe that "the free world won not only the Cold War but the war of ideas. Socialism is no longer fashionable; today's cutting-edge ideas involve the institutions of freedom: property rights, contracts, the rule of law and freedom of conscience and expression."

"What ails conservatism these days," Postrel and Glassman assert, "is that many conservatives, especially in Washington, are deeply alienated from American life." Rejecting pleas to "American Greatness" through activist government, they urge that "Americans don't need to concoct grand national struggles merely to prove their mettle. They prove it every day, in their own private pursuits."

Conservatives William Kristol and David Brooks agree with many of the latter points. "What's missing from today's American conservatism is America," they write, also in the *Journal*. "The gravest threat to America today," they argue, "is the complacent mediocrity and petty meddling of the nanny state."

But many problems in our society require aggressive government action—not to enlarge the nanny state, but to decentralize power to people and communities. Their prescription:

> Today this means policies that would bust the great trusts of
> our time—the education, health and Social Security monopolies.

It means welfare programs that demand personal responsibility. It means education policies that promote high standards, challenge our best students, and promote scientific and national progress. It means taking seriously questions of public morality, while recognizing the limitations of legal sanctions.[6]

Who is right: Postrel and Glassman, or Kristol and Brooks? The answer is both. Though presented as a sharp disagreement, the debate between libertarians and conservatives yields important consensus themes. Individual autonomy, free enterprise, and private property are the keys to freedom, prosperity, and progress. The state cannot enforce subjective moral edicts without violating freedom. Yet the state, in everything it does, invariably affects private behavior. It ought to do as little harm as possible, and to encourage constructive behavior rather than destructive social pathologies. And most important, it must act aggressively to remove barriers to opportunity that government itself has erected, so that all individuals may pursue the American Dream.

If much of this seems hopelessly abstract or reductively optimistic, one need only examine what is going on in the real world. At its core, this book is a clarion call to step outside the rarefied world of academia, think tanks, media, and politics and venture out into the everyday world. There we will find desperate, seemingly intractable problems—and often, readily apparent solutions; not from Washington, not from establishment civil rights groups, but from the people themselves. And we will discover, to the surprise of many, that the American Dream still burns bright in the hearts of people who have endured the greatest hardships.

In an insightful recent article in the *Los Angeles Times*, Ronald Brownstein observes that "[i]t's easy to despair over the state of the cities. Despite the dramatic national reductions in crime and unemployment, many inner-city neighborhoods remain bereft of both order and opportunity. Even in a rising tide, some of these corners seem anchored in hopelessness." But, he adds,

[L]ook closer and a different picture emerges. In Boston, the Ten-Point Coalition—an alliance of black ministers—has spearheaded a remarkable reduction in youth violence. In New York, the Mid-Bronx Desperadoes Community Housing Corp. has converted streets that once symbolized decay into rows of sturdy homes for working families. And in San Antonio, a religion-based drug-treatment service known as Teen Challenge has shown real gains in treating young addicts.[7]

"Top-down solutions ultimately will be rejected," says the Rev. Jeffrey L. Brown, pastor of the Union Baptist Church in Cambridge, Massachusetts. "The only things that work are the things that come from the bottom up, one person at a time, one day at a time." Concludes Ronald Brownstein, "Local action can't substitute for national commitment. But these ideas embody the insight that supporting local action can be the best means of expressing national commitment."

Robert L. Woodson, Sr., puts crisply the prescription for empowerment:

> We must admit the real experts are in the neighborhoods that experience the problems. To remain reliant on elitist specialists and professionals for our answers is to invite failure. An agenda of empowerment must replace an opportunist-ridden system of "custodianship," and programs should be targeted, exclusively, to those who are most in need.[8]

Among Washington-based advocates, my colleagues and I at the Institute for Justice are unusual and very lucky in working every day with people outside the Beltway who are striving, despite the odds, to earn a share of the American Dream. They come up with the solutions; we supply the legal tools to challenge the red tape and the special interests that too often prevent such solutions from taking shape. Public policy should nurture such efforts, empowering people to control their own destinies. In the pages that follow, I draw upon cutting-edge ideas from thinkers from all parts of the political spectrum, but more significantly, from the real experiences of real people. It is from their lessons that we can help others find their way to the true opportunities that are every American's birthright.

That so many among us cannot realistically aspire to the pursuit of happiness is a blight on America's soul. But amidst the rubble of failed policies and social pathologies, the light of hope burns brightly. The moral obligation of every American is to honor the promise of opportunity for all. We urgently need to roll up our sleeves and work toward making our common destiny an America where everyone has the chance to achieve to the utmost limits of his or her talents and aspirations.

1

GRIM REALITIES[1]

I don't have to look at a film of children from a third-world country. We have that same misery here.

— Hannah M. Hawkins, Director,
Children of Mine, Washington, D.C.[2]

America remains a land of opportunity. Each year tens of thousands of newcomers enter our country. They come not to join the welfare rolls, but to earn a share of the American Dream. Go to a California vineyard and you will see them working the soil, go to a Fairfax County, Virginia public library on a Saturday and you will see their children studying, go to cities across the nation and you will see them performing jobs that native-born Americans don't want, visit Silicon Valley and you will see them contributing highly-honed technical skills to the American economy. In many ways, the newcomers are more American than many people who were born here: most are patriotic, honest, hard-working, family-oriented. Many of them risk their lives or make enormous sacrifices to come to the land of opportunity. They reap the benefits of a system that still rewards those virtues and they enrich our society.

Yet tragically, America has not made those same opportunities available to many of its own native-born citizens. Within our midst live millions of people so mired in poverty and negative pathologies that they may never climb out. As the great social scientist James Q. Wilson has observed, America today is not one nation but two:

> In one nation, a child, raised by two parents, acquires an education, a job, a spouse, and a home kept separate from crime and disorder by distance, fences, or guards. In the other nation, a child is raised by an unwed girl, lives in a neighborhood filled with many sexual men but few committed fathers, and finds gang life to be necessary for self-protection and valuable for self-advancement. In the first nation, children look to the future and believe that they control what place they will occupy in it; in the second, they live for the moment and think that fate, not plans, will shape their lives. In both nations, harms occur, but in the second they proliferate— child abuse and drug abuse, gang violence and personal criminality, economic dependency and continued illegitimacy.[3]

This poverty and mass social dislocation in the midst of plenty is not the fault of American stinginess or a failure to redistribute wealth; indeed, it exists not merely despite public policy interventions but in large part because of them. After four decades of massive income redistribution, even some liberals now concede that such efforts cannot produce equal outcomes.[4] Yet we have focused on redistribution to the exclusion of removing barriers to basic opportunities. The route to prosperity in America is no secret: generation after generation has advanced through education and enterprise. We guarantee no outcomes here, but we do guarantee equal opportunity—the one sacred promise that Americans have made to each other since the Declaration of Independence. It is the failure to deliver on the promise of opportunity for many of the people who most need it that presents the greatest dilemma in public policy today.

Conditions of unequal opportunity are visited disproportionately upon poor, minority, inner-city people. Not all people who are poor or who live in inner cities suffer such conditions, nor do most minority individuals. But for millions who share those characteristics, the burdens are so great that the pursuit of happiness is illusory. They are isolated from the basic opportunities that most other people take for granted: they cannot get their children a good education, they cannot earn a legitimate livelihood, they cannot walk the streets safely at night, and the community support structures that might help them out of all that are eroded.

In particular, these conditions disproportionately afflict black Americans. Blacks have experienced unique deprivations throughout American history, and progress has been uneven. Because the people who are mired in urban poverty are disproportionately black, their circumstances contribute to the racial disparities that so-called civil rights advocates wave around to prove endemic racism and the need for race-based remedies. But the most-disadvantaged people benefit not at all from such remedies, for typically they are not in a position to compete for preferential college admissions or professional opportunities, race-based contract set-asides, or other elite privileges.[5] Those policies are what I call "trickle-down civil rights"—policies that confer enormous benefits based on racial "disadvantage" yet somehow never reach their purported beneficiaries.[6]

"We need to define affirmative action for what it is," says Robert L. Woodson. "If it is a remedy that helps middle and upper income blacks, that's fine. If it's a middle-income entitlement, let's call it that. But don't use all blacks as the rationale for implementing something that benefits a few."[7] Low-income people are used by liberals and ignored by most conservatives, while all the time their circumstances grow more dire. The isolation of so many people in our midst from the reality of equal opportunities is the greatest tragedy in America today.

That is not to understate the enormous strides America has made in recent years in making good on the promise of opportunity for many who previously were denied it. In 1944, Swedish sociologist Gunnar Myrdal concluded in his classic treatise *The American Dilemma* that "the color line" was the central vexing issue in American life and public policy.[8] In their magnificent recent book *America in Black and White*, Stephan and Abigail Thernstrom revisit much of the territory explored by Myrdal, and conclude that of late, "the bad news has been exaggerated, and the good news has been neglected."[9] Michael Meyers of the New York Civil Rights

Commission agrees. "This is a good time for a lot of people," he says. "You can't argue against the facts. We have made a whole lot of progress in race relations, and we have to acknowledge that."[10]

Good news is abundant, and has proliferated fairly rapidly. In the early 1940s, 87 percent of blacks lived below the poverty line, and 64 percent of black women worked as domestic servants.[11] By contrast, less than a half-century later, four out of ten blacks today consider themselves middle-class.[12] The percentage of black families with incomes at least twice the poverty line has grown from a mere 1 percent in 1940 to 49 percent today (compared to 75 percent for whites).[13] The median income for black married-couple families in 1995 was $41,307—87 percent of the average income for white married-couple families.[14]

Educationally, too, black Americans are progressing: in 1980, only 51.2 percent of blacks over the age of twenty-five had completed four years of high school; by 1995, that proportion had increased to 73.8 percent—and to 86.5 percent among blacks between twenty-five and twenty-nine years of age.[15] College attendance is up, too, from 21.9 percent of blacks in 1980 to 37.5 percent in 1995.[16] Those gains are important because education correlates highly with income, and the income gap between blacks and whites closes progressively with advanced education. Black women who have graduated high school, attended some college, or graduated from college all earn *more* money, on average, than their white female counterparts.[17]

Meanwhile, the proportion of blacks living in the suburbs has grown from 22.3 percent in 1980 to 31.9 percent in 1995.[18] Americans are living and interacting more frequently across racial lines: in 1960, only 20 percent of whites reported blacks living in their neighborhoods, but by 1994, 61 percent did; 83 percent of blacks report whites living in their neighborhoods.[19] The proportion of blacks who have at least one good white friend grew from 21 percent in 1975 to 78 percent in 1994, and the proportion of whites who have at least one good black friend soared from 9 to 73 percent in the same 20-year span.[20] Interracial dating and marriages have increased substantially.[21]

Still, despite improvements in race relations, troublesome signs of alienation persist. Perhaps no better indication of differing views of the world was the polar-opposite reaction among whites and blacks to the

O. J. Simpson verdict: immediately following the trial, only 17 percent of blacks would have voted to convict, and only 18 percent of whites would have voted to acquit.[22] A 1989 survey found that 26 percent of blacks believed that most whites shared the views of the Ku Klux Klan; another 25 percent of blacks believed at least one-quarter of whites harbored such sympathies. Asked in 1993, only 44 percent of blacks thought a solution could be worked out to the race problem—a remarkable decline of twenty-six percentage points since 1963, the year before passage of the Civil Rights Act.[23] Meanwhile, the race-based policies ostensibly designed to bring the races together have, not surprisingly, widened the chasm. In their pathbreaking analysis of race relations *The Scar of Race*, political scientists Paul M. Sniderman and Thomas Piazza found that race-conscious government policies induce negative stereotypes of blacks—among *both* whites and blacks.[24]

Pessimism and alienation are all too understandable, for the bad news is grave. The following statistics distill the picture with shocking clarity:

- The National Urban League projects that by the close of the century, 76 percent of black children will be born out of wedlock.[25]
- In 1995, the National Assessment of Educational Progress reported that only 12 percent of black high school seniors were proficient in reading.[26]
- A study released in 1995 showed that one out of every three black men between the ages of twenty and twenty-nine was in jail or otherwise under the supervision of the criminal justice system.[27] At the same time, blacks are 6.4 times more likely to die by homicide than whites.[28]

Each of these statistics is grim. Together they are devastating. And given those grim realities, what is surprising is not that we see significant racial disparities in most indicia of life success, but rather that those disparities are not much larger.

Writing recently in the *Omaha World-Herald*, Stephen Buttry observes that "[w]hatever progress has been made in fighting racial discrimination and in increasing opportunities for blacks, life generally remains vastly different for blacks than for whites." He catalogues some of the obstacles a typical black person will face:

Starting before birth, a black child faces longer odds against survival and success than a white child.

Black women are more likely than white women to become pregnant without marrying, to have abortions, to delay or forego prenatal care. At birth, the child faces a life expectancy that is seven years shorter than a white baby's.

The bleak outlook continues through life. . . . Especially if the child is a boy, he is more likely than a white child to die as a baby, as an adolescent and as a young adult. He is more likely to drop out of school, be arrested, go to prison, contract AIDS, be murdered.

The black child, even if she is a girl, is less likely to finish high school, college or graduate school, less apt to use computers, less likely to have health insurance or visit the doctor unless it's an emergency. [29]

Given the enormous progress that many black Americans have made in the past half-century, how can those conditions persist among so many others? The fact is that progress has been dramatically uneven. University of Chicago sociologist William Julius Wilson points out that while real incomes were rising by 23 percent for the wealthiest one-fifth of blacks between 1975 and 1992—and by 35 percent for the wealthiest 5 percent of blacks—incomes for the poorest one-fifth of blacks *declined* by 33 percent, and declined by 13 percent for the second-poorest one-fifth of blacks.[30] Overall, in 1995, 29.3 percent of blacks—and an even-higher 30.3 percent of Hispanics—lived beneath the poverty line, compared to only 8.5 percent of non-Hispanic whites.[31] The black-to-white unemployment ratio, which remained fairly constant at about 2 to 1 throughout the 1960s and 1970s, rose steadily in the 1980s until it had grown to 2.76 to 1 by 1990.[32]

Part of the explanation, Wilson explains, is that despite an increase in black suburbanization, there has been a "growing concentration of minority residents in the most impoverished areas of the nation's metropolises."[33] Partly as a result of overall urban population losses, the proportion of the population that is black in New York City increased from 14 to 29 percent between 1960 and 1990, from 23 to 39 percent in Chicago, from 54 to 66 percent in the District of Columbia, and from 29 to 76 percent in Detroit.[34] The vast majority of people in urban ghettoes—seven out of eight—are minorities. Overall, the number of blacks living in urban ghettoes increased by one-third between 1980 and 1990 to six million.[35] At the same time, poverty has concentrated in large cities: in 1959, less than one-third of the poverty population in the United States lived in central cities; today, close to one-half does.[36] Meanwhile, even as some commercial centers have enjoyed a renaissance, the central cities have deteriorated starkly.[37]

The concentration and isolation of many minorities within urban ghettoes have substantial adverse consequences. As Wilson explains, "ghetto-related behaviors often represent particular cultural adaptations to the systematic blockage of opportunities in the environment of the inner city and the society as a whole. These adaptations are reflected in habits, skills, styles, and attitudes that are shaped over time."[38]

Perhaps most devastating is the explosive growth in numbers of out-of-wedlock births. William Galson, former senior policy advisor to President Clinton and now a professor at the University of Maryland, notes that people need do only three things to avoid poverty in America: finish high school, marry before bearing children, and have children after age twenty. Of those who do, only 8 percent are poor; of those who fail to do those things, 79 percent are poor.[39] The problem, as the Thernstroms observe, is that today "[m]any fewer black women are marrying, and yet they continue to have children—which was not the case in an earlier era."[40] The percentage of black children born out of wedlock rose from 22 percent in 1960 to 38 percent in 1970, and soared to 70 percent in 1994. (The out-of-wedlock birth rate among whites also increased from 2 percent in 1960 to 25 percent in 1994.)[41] As a result of those trends, despite an overall increase in black affluence, the percentage of black children in poverty grew from 40 percent in 1969 to 42 percent in 1995. Among black children in poverty, 62 percent live in female-headed households.[42] The economic consequences of out-of-wedlock births and low marriage rates are devastating: while the 1993 median income of married-couple black families was $43,578, it was only $9,272 for families headed by never-married mothers.[43]

Children born out of wedlock experience diminished opportunities throughout their lives. As the Heritage Foundation's Patrick F. Fagan reports, children born out of wedlock on average suffer poorer health as newborns and have an increased chance of dying young, experience retarded cognitive development, can expect lower educational achievement and job and income attainment, engage in increased behavioral problems, and are more likely to become long-term welfare recipients and to give birth to out-of-wedlock children.[44] As the rate of black single-parent families increases—with the trajectory expected to rise to perhaps three-fourths of all black children born at the turn of the next century—attendant pathologies of dependency, low educational attainments, unemployment, and criminality will likely grow as well.

With respect to education, the situation is mixed. The good news about vastly increased rates of high-school graduation and college attendance among blacks mask problems beneath the surface. In 1995, the percentage of blacks ages twenty-five to twenty-nine who had graduated from high school fell by more than two percentage points, even as the percentage of whites who graduated increased.[45] College attrition is an almost epidemic problem. Although over one-third of blacks over age twenty-five have attended college, only 13.2 percent of blacks have graduated from college. In other words, only one in three black college students graduate, compared to more than 70 percent of whites.[46] The staggering college dropout rate for blacks seems to correlate, perversely, with preferential admissions policies: postsecondary institutions that provide greater adjustments for blacks in their admissions credentials generally also experience higher dropout rates among black students.[47] What seems to be happening is that the widespread practice of adding points to black college applicants' test scores is creating a mismatch between students and schools, and the high dropout rates illustrate the cost exacted by policies that emphasize preferences rather than skills.

Even more troublesome is the large and growing racial achievement gap among high school students, which was closing substantially during the 1980s but has widened since. In 1980, black seventeen-year-olds were six academic years behind their white counterparts on the reading portion of the National Assessment of Educational Progress. By 1988, the gap had narrowed to 2.5 years—but by 1994 it had grown again to 3.9 years. In math, the gap widened from 2.5 years in 1990 to 3.4 years in 1994; and it has increased as well in science (5.4 years) and writing

(3.3 years).[48] The prognosis is bleak: as long as blacks who graduate from high school are roughly four academic years behind white students, we will surely continue to see enormous disparities in college admissions and graduation as well as professional attainments. That problem has not been addressed, and indeed it has been swept under the carpet of racial preferences.

A third blight is crime, in which blacks and inner-city dwellers are represented disproportionately both as perpetrators and victims. Whereas one-third of young black men are under judicial supervision nationally, that number is even higher in large cities. In 1997, the National Center on Institutions and Alternatives reported that 50 percent of all black men between the ages of eighteen and thirty-five in the District of Columbia were in jail or otherwise under the custody of the criminal justice system, up from 42 percent five years earlier.[49] Even more pronounced is the likelihood of being victimized by crime: in only seven years between 1984 and 1991, the homicide rate for black males between the ages of fourteen and seventeen more than tripled from 32 to 112 per 100,000—more than eight times the rate for white males in the same age bracket.[50]

Take any one of those statistics—out-of-wedlock births, education, and crime—and we see people in serious trouble. Take all three together and they spell a cycle of crisis. And yet this cycle takes place in the midst of unprecedented economic prosperity—prosperity that includes many blacks. Millions of blacks and other minority individuals have solidly entered the mainstream of American life. Yet millions more are further isolated than ever before.

Those widely divergent trends—progress alongside crisis—suggest that on issues of race and opportunity, though we have much to celebrate, we also have much left to do. The statistics demonstrate further that the problems facing us as we approach the millennium are different than they were in the 1950s and '60s. In some instances, such as overt racism, the problems are not as bad as they once were. In other cases, such as crime, education, and community disintegration, they are worse—much worse. That means the tools designed to redress problems in the 1950s and '60s are not tailored to the realities of the 1990s and beyond. As Richard D. Kahlenberg points out in his provocative book *The Remedy*, race is no longer a proxy for disadvantage.[51] Whatever their past efficacy, race-based public policies are too crude to have much effectiveness today in delivering help to people who most need it.

Meanwhile, traditional minority-oriented organizations seem caught in a time warp, relics of a time gone by. By treating symptoms rather than root causes, they have done little to address the real problems that lead to wide racial achievement gaps. Inevitably, they attribute such disparities to racism, and deploy tools ostensibly designed to remedy discrimination. To disdain their redistributionist agenda and hysterical rhetoric is not to belittle the problem of racism, which remains all too prevalent in American society. The civil rights laws were necessary to level the playing field, and they remain so. But they are hopelessly inadequate to redress the problems of people who are outside the economic mainstream. The sad fact is that if racism disappeared tomorrow, the combined effects of soaring numbers of out-of-wedlock births, educational deprivations, and high rates of crime would conspire to prevent significant black progress. As Katherine Kersten observed recently in the *Minneapolis Star Tribune*, many of today's "social pathologies were barely on the radar screen in the 1950s, when racism was far more widespread than it is today."[52]

Moreover, tools designed to combat racism are ill-suited to address the underlying problems afflicting low-income minorities. President Clinton has admitted as much, commenting that affirmative action "doesn't reach the vast majority of the people who have a problem because it doesn't reach down into basically the isolated urban areas with people in the economic underclass."[53] Likewise, as William Julius Wilson has observed repeatedly, race-conscious "policies of affirmative action are likely to enhance opportunities for the more advantaged without adequately remedying the problems of the disadvantaged."[54] A race-based set-aside, racial preferences in college admissions, and hiring preferences cannot, by definition, benefit those who cannot even reach the starting gate.

In light of all that, we badly need to resist the snake-oil prescriptions peddled by the likes of Jesse Jackson, the National Association for the Advancement of Colored People, and other so-called civil rights leaders and groups. Reprehensibly, many of them campaign for divisive racial entitlements for middle- and upper-class minorities in the names of those who will never reap the benefits of such trickle-down civil rights.[55] Race-based policies are worse than irrelevant for the people at the bottom, for they provide the false cosmetic appearance that we are solving problems of racial disparities when in fact the underlying causes are ignored and continue to fester. Meanwhile, when promising solutions are proposed to help poor people help themselves, establishment civil rights groups typically are nowhere to be found—or worse, as in the case of the NAACP's opposition to school choice, they are on the wrong side, working against their purported constituents.

As William Julius Wilson concludes, "Without disavowing the accomplishments of the civil rights movement, black leaders and policy makers now need to give more attention to remedies that will make a concrete difference in the lives of the poor."[56] We desperately need to attend to that task. We cannot abide a society divided between those who have access to basic opportunities and those who do not. As Rev. Martin Luther King, Jr. declared on the steps of the Lincoln Memorial:

> When the architects of our republic wrote the magnificent words of the Constitution and Declaration of Independence, they were signing a promissory note to which every American would fall heir. This note was a promise that all men, yes black men as well as white men, would be guaranteed the unalienable rights of life, liberty, and the pursuit of happiness.[57]

Now is the time to redeem that promise.

2

BLACKS AND WHITES ON COMMON GROUND

*One day we will win freedom, but not only for our-
selves. We shall so appeal to your heart and conscience
that we shall win you in the process, and our victory will be
a double victory.*

—Rev. Martin Luther King, Jr.[1]

Blacks and whites have vastly different historical experiences in
America. Many still find themselves in starkly different
circumstances today. Polls suggest that while both blacks and
whites believe our nation has made real racial progress, both groups also
believe that race problems will endure. Given those differences, is there a
possible set of shared values upon which we can construct a unifying consensus and a positive new approach to issues of race and opportunity?

The answer is yes. It is based on what Gunnar Myrdal called the
"American Creed": the "ideals of the essential dignity of the individual
human being, of the fundamental equality of all men, and of certain
inalienable rights to freedom, justice, and a fair opportunity."[2] The
creed traces back, of course, to the Declaration of Independence, which
recognized the equal rights of all individuals; and its principles carried
forward through the crusade to abolish slavery and the adoption of

the Fourteenth Amendment, to *Brown v. Board of Education* and the modern civil rights movement. Adherence to the creed has fueled every great civil rights triumph; deviations from the creed have produced racial division and conflict.[3]

In his sociological exploration of American race relations in the 1940s, Myrdal marveled over how strong the American Creed remained among blacks despite generations of racism and oppression. Honoring the creed, he urged, was the surest means by which America could finally heal its racial divide. Through the mid-1960s, civil rights leaders understood the importance of the American Creed. In particular, Rev. Martin Luther King, Jr. repeatedly invoked the historical underpinnings and universality of the American Creed.[4] But the emergence of the massive Great Society welfare state, along with other redistributionist policies that perpetuated racial classifications in law and public policy, marked a sharp departure from the principles of individualism and equality under law that girded the American Creed.

Still, the American Creed remains alive in the hearts and minds of the people, black and white, rich and poor. As in Myrdal's day more than a half-century ago, it is the creed—the dream—that holds the greatest promise to heal the social and economic chasms that divide Americans.

In light of the identification of many minorities and the poor with liberal politics, the extent to which many poor and minority individuals adhere to traditional American values, such as hard work and individual responsibility, may come as a surprise. "Despite the over-whelming poverty," remarks William Julius Wilson, "black residents in inner-city ghetto neighborhoods verbally reinforce, rather than under-mine, the basic American values pertaining to individual initiative."[5]

My colleagues and I constantly find that observation true. Most middle-class Americans derive their impressions about life in the inner cities from television, which paints vivid images of criminals, drug addicts, and welfare recipients. What one encounters more frequently in real life are people not much different from their suburban counter-parts in their aspirations and values, but enmeshed in vastly different circumstances. Poor people in the inner cities want the same things for themselves and their families as do other Americans: a nice home in a safe neighborhood, financial security, good schools. Like middle-class Americans, most poor people in inner cities understand that the only sure means to real success in life is education and hard work. The main difference is that for many such people, the path from here to there is blocked by huge obstacles and perverse incentives.

Equally surprising to the casual observer is the extent to which the views of mainstream minority individuals on important issues of public policy diverge dramatically from those of groups and leaders who claim to speak for them. Jesse Jackson, Al Sharpton, Willie Brown, Maxine Waters, and their ilk grab the headlines, but mainstream black Americans tend to hold much more conservative views and values. Those traditional ideals provide the strongest basis for common ground between whites and blacks.

We must reclaim that common ground. America is fast becoming an increasingly diverse nation in which no true "majority" group exists. In 1995, whites (who themselves, of course, are extremely heterogeneous) accounted for 74 percent of the nation's population; blacks made up 12 percent, Hispanics 10 percent, Asians 3 percent. In only a dozen years from now, the proportion of whites will be only 67 percent of America's population; the proportion of blacks will increase to 13 percent, Hispanics to 14 percent, Asians to 5 percent. In the year 2050, whites will account for barely half the nation's population; Hispanics will increase to 26 percent, blacks to 14 percent, and Asians to 8 percent.[6]

Given those demographic trends, it is clear that America will either become even more ethnically Balkanized than it is now, or unite once again behind a common set of values and principles. Commenting on alienation among many blacks—which, peculiarly, seems most pronounced among successful blacks—Cinqué Henderson offers this insightful prescription:

> This entire phenomenon rests on the acceptance of the racist assumption that blacks are separate from the whole of society, even as we are part of it—a limb that may be easily amputated. As long as black people continue to accept (and white racists and black racialists continue to perpetuate) the idea that we are ancillary members of this country, that we can be ghettoized or segregated out of existence, we will forever doubt our place here.[7]

All of America's people, including its minorities and immigrants, must be welcomed as full partners in the American experiment.

Polling on many issues and values suggests a broad base for the common ground necessary to make that happen. Even as whites and, to a greater extent, blacks continue to despair over solutions to race issues, both groups share common core beliefs, aspirations, and views on essential questions of public policy.

A first salient point is that despite their strong affiliation with the Democratic Party, blacks are not monolithically liberal. Far from it. A 1996 poll by the liberal Joint Center for Political and Economic Studies found blacks are evenly distributed across the ideological spectrum: 30 percent label themselves conservative, 31 percent liberal, and 32 percent moderate.[8] Likewise, although Hispanics increasingly align with Democrats, they are more conservative than most Americans on social issues such as abortion and crime. Hispanics also have a strong and growing culture of small-business entrepreneurship.[9]

Blacks and whites generally assign importance to the same issues. The two groups identify different top national priorities: in late 1996, the Polling Company found that a plurality of whites (31 percent) considered cutting government spending and balancing the budget the number one national priority, compared to only 16 percent of blacks (who ranked the issue third).[10] Both groups, however, ranked education and fighting crime and drugs as high priorities. A large plurality of blacks—42 percent—ranked improving education as the top priority, compared to 25 percent of whites (who overall ranked it second). Twenty-one percent of blacks and 17 percent of whites said that fighting crime and drugs is the top national priority.

On welfare, views of whites and blacks are highly convergent. A 1992 poll by the Joint Center for Political and Economic Studies found that 57 percent of blacks oppose increasing welfare payments when recipients have more children.[11] The National Black Election Study found that 64 percent of blacks support the five-year lifetime limit on welfare benefits contained in recent federal welfare reform legislation.[12] Although House Speaker Newt Gingrich was criticized for his suggestion that the government place children from dangerous homes in orphanages, the Joint Center found in June 1997 that the idea was supported by 81.4 percent of Hispanics, 75.5 percent of blacks, and 61.1 percent of whites.[13]

Blacks on average are more concerned than whites about crime because the issue more often hits close to home. The Center for New Black Leadership reports that in 1994, 57 percent of blacks reported that "there were places where they were afraid to walk alone at night."[14] Those fears translate into conservative, tough-on-crime views. A 1993 poll found that 59 percent of blacks favor eliminating parole for violent offenders, and 58 percent support the death penalty for murderers.[15] Seventy-three percent of blacks support "three-strikes-and-out" sentencing rules.[16]

Issues of education provide perhaps the best opportunity for common ground. Majorities of both whites and blacks attribute differences in income between the races to a lack of educational opportunities for blacks.[17] As noted previously, black Americans consider education the most important issue; but they also are more likely than whites to view their schools as poor in quality and to favor systemic reform. According to the 1997 Joint Center survey, only 30 percent of blacks and 39.4 percent of Hispanics rated their public schools "excellent" or "good," compared to 60.7 percent of whites. By contrast, 64.3 percent of blacks and 60.6 percent of Hispanics rated their public schools "fair" or "poor," contrasted with 35.7 percent of whites.[18] Support for school vouchers is most intense among Hispanics and blacks. The Joint Center found that while whites are evenly split, Hispanics favor school choice by 65.4 to 28.6 percent and blacks by 55.8 percent to 37.5 percent. Among blacks, the poll found, support was highest among those in the age bracket most likely to have school-age children: 86.5 percent of blacks ages twenty-six to thirty-five support school choice, while only 10.3 percent oppose it.[19]

On those central issues—welfare, crime, and education—black Americans are far more conservative than the groups that purport to represent minority interests.[20] A survey by Linda Lichter found a remarkable gulf between mainstream black Americans and leaders of black organizations on a variety of issues. For instance, 68 percent of black organization leaders supported busing for racial integration, even though a majority of blacks opposed it. Likewise, two-thirds of black leaders opposed capital punishment, while a majority of mainstream blacks favored it.[21]

Those findings square with overt actions taken against the interests and views of minority Americans by groups that ostensibly represent them. Hispanic groups, for instance, are actively fighting efforts by Hispanic parents to get their kids into classes that will teach them English.[22] The NAACP Legal Defense Fund actively seeks to end capital punishment even though most blacks support it and blacks are disproportionately victimized by homicides. The NAACP fought a five-year time limit for welfare benefits, even though nearly two-thirds of blacks supported it.[23] And despite overwhelming black support for school choice—and the fact that the vast majority of school choice beneficiaries are black—the NAACP has challenged the Milwaukee program in court and has joined with People for the American Way to fight school choice nationally. Not surprisingly, many blacks have turned away from establishment special interest organizations like the NAACP toward community-based fraternal, professional, and mentoring groups, many of which have a self-help focus, and which provided the backbone of the Million Man March in 1995.[24]

The main and fundamental difference between blacks and whites is their respective views toward government intervention to improve social and economic conditions, a phenomenon to which I will turn in chapter 7. A 1995 poll found that 70 percent of blacks, but only 38 percent of whites, believed that the federal government can help blacks solve severe problems. A poll the previous year found that 74 percent of blacks believed that too little government aid is given to blacks, while only 16 percent of whites agreed.[25] An overwhelming majority of blacks—about 86 percent—believe too little government money is spent to assist the poor, whereas barely 50 percent of whites agree. (Curiously, only about 30 percent of blacks think too little is spent on welfare, compared to about 10 percent of whites, suggesting that a large majority of both blacks and whites think welfare is not an effective means of aiding poor people.) Nearly 45 percent of black Americans believe that the government should take steps to reduce income differences between rich and poor, while only about 20 percent of whites agree. Notably, black support for such intervention has declined by about ten percentage points over the past decade.[26]

How do the differing perspectives over the proper role of government translate into the most contentious race-related issue, racial preferences and affirmative action? At first blush, the racial divide over this issue seems intractable. The most sophisticated polling suggests that people have strongly-held views on racial preferences that are not likely to change over time.[27] Blacks and whites split deeply over California's Proposition 209, which outlawed race and gender preferences by state and local government. Wide disagreement exists over affirmative action and related policies no matter how the issues are presented. But even on this incendiary issue, public opinion polls suggest a possible common ground: against racial preferences, yet in favor of "affirmative action" that does not discriminate on the basis of race and gender.

First and foremost, a huge majority of all Americans, whites and blacks alike, believe it remains necessary to have laws protecting minorities against discrimination.[28] Beyond that basic agreement, a strong consensus exists, even among many blacks, that preferential policies are unfair. Polls consistently find that a large majority of Americans oppose race and gender preferences. A 1997 *New York Times* poll found that 52 percent of all Americans are opposed to preferences to make up for past discrimination, while 35 percent favor preferences. Whites opposed preferences by 62 to 23 percent, while blacks favored them by 57 to 31 percent.[29] Asking the question differently, the Joint Center for Political and Economic Studies in 1997 found that only 18.9 percent of Americans agree that "we should make every possible effort to improve the position of blacks and other minorities, even if it means giving them preferential treatment," while 78.7 percent disagree. Although black and white opinions diverged markedly on that question, a plurality of blacks—48.8 percent—disagreed with preferential treatment, while 45.3 percent supported it. Among Hispanics, 53.8 percent opposed preferential treatment while 41.9 percent supported it. Whites opposed it by 83 to 15.3 percent.[30] Those findings indicate that although blacks and whites have differences over racial preferences, many (if not most) blacks agree with a large majority of their fellow Americans that preferences are wrong.

But while most are opposed to preferences, many Americans are more favorable toward "affirmative action." The *New York Times* poll found that 47 percent of all Americans—including 52 percent of whites and 14 percent of blacks—believe that affirmative action should be abolished, while 41 percent of all Americans—including 80 percent of blacks and 35 percent of whites—believe it should not.[31] Prior polls showed even stronger support for affirmative action, at the same time Americans opposed race and gender preferences.[32]

The only possible explanation for those disparate results is that many Americans perceive a difference between preferences and affirmative action—even though the vast majority of contemporary affirmative action programs involve preferences. This distinction is buttressed by responses to other questions posed by the *New York Times* poll. Majorities in excess of 60 percent of all respondents—including majorities of whites—supported "outreach," training, and education efforts to increase the pool of qualified minority candidates and to help minorities compete. Likewise, 53 percent of all respondents favored "affirmative action" programs targeted to the poor in the event such programs are abolished for minorities, compared to 37 percent who oppose such "socioeconomic" affirmative action.[33]

These findings suggest two areas of broad and enduring consensus that bridge the racial divide. First, most people believe that programs that confer preferential treatment on the basis of race or gender are unfair and should be abolished. Second, efforts to enlarge the pool of qualified applicants—without discrimination—or to help people who are truly disadvantaged, are strongly supported. Those points of consensus agree with deeply-held American principles: that discrimination is wrong, no matter what euphemism is used to describe it; but that we should extend a helping hand to people who truly need it.

There appears no strong consensus, however, behind massive new social engineering or wealth redistribution schemes. Many of the activists who are fighting to abolish race and gender preferences understandably are suspicious about new "affirmative action" programs based on disadvantage or other factors, even if preferential treatment is forbidden.[34] Such programs ought to be debated on a case-by-case basis. For instance, the Small Business Administration section 8(a) program is supposed to target loans to "socially and economically disadvantaged individuals," but in fact has operated as a race and gender preference program. If such preferences are abolished, the program for the first time will have to target aid exclusively to people who are disadvantaged, such as start-up entrepreneurs in poor inner-city neighborhoods. Likewise, it makes sense for public colleges to assist students who have overcome special obstacles, such as coming from single-parent families or the first generation to attend college, categories that disproportionately encompass blacks and Hispanics.

Defenders of racial preferences argue against targeting affirmative action on the basis of disadvantage, correctly claiming that the largest number of Americans living in poverty are whites, not blacks. Indeed, 1995 Census Bureau statistics show that 44.7 percent of people below the poverty level were white, 27.1 percent were black, 22.4 percent were Hispanic, and 5.8 percent were other races.[35] But poverty afflicts minorities much more severely than whites: in 1995, 30.3 percent of Hispanics and 29.3 percent of blacks were below the poverty level, compared with 14.6 percent of Asians and 8.5 percent of whites.[36] Furthermore, blacks and Hispanics are much more likely to be concentrated in urban ghettoes, where conditions converge to reinforce poverty. Hence, efforts to help people lift themselves out of poverty will disproportionately benefit disadvantaged minority individuals. Although the Milwaukee Parental Choice Program, for example, provides school vouchers on the basis of city residency and income, 96 percent of the vouchers are used by black and Hispanic children.

The goals of future efforts to aid the poor should be to provide the tools necessary to compete and to eliminate barriers to opportunity. A strong common ground buttresses that approach, extending even to many liberals. A 1997 poll by the Democratic Leadership Council asked Democrats the best way to promote racial equality. Only 14 percent identified affirmative action programs, while 25 percent identified improving inner-city schools, 12 percent identified reducing crime through more and better policing, and a 39 percent plurality identified empowering low-income minorities to work and start businesses.[37]

It seems, then, that two main tasks await those who desire to narrow the racial divide and to make good on the promise of equal opportunity. The first is to promote a philosophy of individualism. As Sniderman and Piazza found in *The Scar of Race*, racism is least pronounced among adherents of individualism, and most pronounced among the poorly educated and those who express authoritarian views.[38] That means that public policy should place less emphasis on racial identity, and greater emphasis on individual merit. Harvard law professor Randall Kennedy puts the point succinctly: "The fact that race matters . . . does not mean that the salience and consequences of racial distinctions are good or that race must continue to matter in the future."[39] To make ours a nation of Americans, we must first treat all our people as Americans.

The second task is to eliminate the artificial barriers that separate people from the basic opportunities that are their birthright as Americans. Ours is a society that remains much too stratified along racial and economic lines. Yet, like middle-class Americans, "people in the inner-city ghetto do internalize the basic American idea that people can get ahead in life if they try," observes William Julius Wilson. "Nonetheless, the social and cultural constraints that confront people in inner-city neighborhoods will cause many who subscribe to these values to fail."[40]

Empowerment is an agenda behind which a majority of Americans, white and black, can unite. The challenge, simply stated, is to remove barriers to opportunity and to empower all Americans to strive and succeed to the outermost limits of their ambition, imagination, and talent. That is America's moral imperative, and its salvation.

3

THE EDUCATION IMPERATIVE

I will find a way to have my children attend private school even if it means less food on the table. A quality education for my children is that important.

—Pilar Gonzalez, Milwaukee parent[1]

One of the hurdles faced by those promoting serious education reform is that the conditions confronting economically disadvantaged children in the inner cities are so shocking and appalling that they stand completely outside the typical American's frame of reference. Imagine schools so dilapidated that their ceilings leak and their windows are boarded up, making them appear long-ago abandoned—except they're bursting at the seams with schoolchildren. Imagine schools so dangerous that authorities have installed metal detectors, teachers are assaulted, and drugs are sold openly on the playgrounds. Imagine schools in which dropout rates exceed 50 percent and a quarter of all students are absent each day, only 12 percent of those who do graduate are proficient in reading and mathematics, and chances of college attendance are virtually nonexistent. Imagine a school system in which the bureaucracy siphons off fifty cents out of every dollar earmarked for education, failing schools cannot be closed or incompetent teachers fired, and where most of the teachers would never enroll their own children.

Things cannot have gotten this bad—except that they have, for low-income youngsters in virtually every large American city. In Cleveland, where I have litigated for the past three years, the numbers 1 in 14 are emblazoned forever upon my memory: children in the Cleveland Public Schools have a 1 in 14 chance of graduating on time and proficient at a senior level—and a 1 in 14 chance each year of being a victim of crime in the schools. When America has reached the point where a poor child has no greater chance to obtain an education than of becoming a crime statistic, we have reached the point of serious crisis. Indeed, the grim reality is that economically disadvantaged children statistically have a far greater chance of joining the welfare rolls or becoming a criminal or a crime victim than of graduating and going on to college or a productive livelihood.

A recent *Los Angeles Times* article by Sheryl Stolberg provides a rare and insightful glimpse into the harsh realities of inner-city public schools. Stolberg profiled Philadelphia's William Penn High School, one of three city schools whose graduates are being tracked as part of an education reform project sponsored by the North Philadelphia Community Compact. As Stolberg describes it, "The noise is deafening, ricocheting off the concrete walls, reverberating, clanging, extinguishing any hope of learning. It sounds like a prison."[2]

But a prison from which it is exceedingly easy to escape to the surrounding streets. Fewer than two of three students attend school each day. Most who attend don't stay long. In 1992, 858 students entered ninth grade at William Penn; on graduation day four years later, only 225 received diplomas. Fifteen percent of the female seniors were pregnant or already mothers; still, girls outnumbered boys 2 to 1 among graduates.

Many of the 225 graduates overcame stupendous odds. David Poe's mother was murdered when he was in the sixth grade. "She always wanted me to finish school," he recounts. "I didn't want to let her down." Michael Leadum took a bullet in a drive-by shooting and spent three months in a wheelchair. Discussing his prospects for the coming year, Michael punctuates it with the caveat, "If I'm still around."

Classmate Tyrone Shoemake was even less lucky, paralyzed for life during a shooting. He still aspires to be an architect, and remarks, "I'm just thankful to be here." Erica Patterson, ranked fourth in her class, shares a two-bedroom apartment with seven other people, including her crack-addicted mother. "Sometimes I want to write a book about my life, about my childhood experiences," Erica remarks. "I think I would call the book *Survive*, or *Survivor*, something like that."[3]

Despite coming so far, prospects are bleak. Among students who take the Scholastic Aptitude Test, the average score for William Penn students is 606 out of 1,600, far below the national average of 902. Tracking graduates from the class of 1993, researchers found that of those who did not go on to college, only 44 percent had jobs six months after graduation. Among the eighty-four graduates who went on to Temple University or the Community College of Philadelphia, fewer than half remained for a second year.

The story of William Penn High School is a microcosm of a nationwide system of educational apartheid, divided along race and especially class lines. More than four decades after *Brown v. Board of Education*, our nation's solemn promise of equal educational opportunities amounts to little more than a cruel hoax for the children who desperately need quality schooling to escape severe conditions of poverty. Minority children are particularly hard hit. As Charles Murray chronicled in his classic *Losing Ground*, by 1980 "the gap in educational achievement between black and white students was so great that it threatened to defeat any other attempts to narrow the economic differences separating blacks and whites."[4] Conditions have not improved since then. The National Assessment of Educational Progress (NAEP) reported in 1995 that only 12 percent of black high school seniors (compared to 40 percent of whites) were proficient in reading.[5] On the 1997 NAEP, 76 percent of white fourth-graders nationwide exhibited basic skills in mathematics, compared to only 41 percent of Hispanic students and 32 percent of black students.[6]

Even worse are dropout rates for minority and poor children. While it is no longer the case that high school graduation alone guarantees work or college, the converse is more true than ever: without a high school diploma, virtually all legitimate avenues of work and higher education are blocked off. Here the statistics are especially grim. Only 70 percent of black students and 50 percent of Hispanic students graduate on time.[7] Dropout rates in inner-city schools are 60 percent. These rates have huge spillover effects: about 90 percent of prison inmates are high school dropouts.[8]

The appalling condition of inner-city public schools reduces enormously the prospects for success among minority individuals and people from economically disadvantaged backgrounds, regardless of race-conscious affirmative action programs. A 1992 study found that "students of high ability and low socioeconomic status are still one-third less likely to enroll [in college] than students of equal ability who come from the highest socioeconomic status."[9] At the graduate level, reports English Professor Nancy Hoffman, "Although the number of institutions searching for African-American candidates has grown significantly, the pool has not." In 1991, only 933 blacks nationwide earned doctoral degrees—a number that actually decreased from 1,013 in 1981.[10] Researcher Sheila Tobias reports that by the year 2000, 30 percent of our nation's youth will be black or Hispanic; but in 1986, only nine blacks or Hispanics earned doctoral degrees in mathematics, and few minority students were pursuing degrees in mathematics.[11] Commenting on the furor over the Fifth Circuit Court of Appeals' decision striking down racial preferences at the University of Texas School of Law,[12] an immigrant District of Columbia cab driver crystallized for me the heart of the matter: "They don't understand the problem is not in college. The problem is in kindergarten."

Defenders of the status quo proffer several explanations for the dismal outcomes. The principal blame, they assert, lies not with the public school system but with the children and their families. Poor children often come from broken families that lack the interest and involvement necessary to buttress the educational process, they contend. And they urge that public schools lack sufficient funds to meet the exceptional needs of low-income urban children. Still others suggest that the problem is racism, which can be solved only by manipulating student assignments to achieve racial balance. And others fret that allowing children to attend private schools will destroy the ideal of "common schooling" that America has tried to build.

Many children in the inner cities do bring severe problems and challenges with them. But those problems are not an excuse for low expectations, which are self-fulfilling. Education, after all, is supposed to provide the surest means to escape impoverished backgrounds. Public schools too often exacerbate problems of poverty rather than relieve them. By contrast, the very same students often thrive in private schools. Much of the problem plainly lies in the system, not in the children it purports to serve.

Likewise, the problem is not insufficient money. Urban school districts typically spend more money per student than statewide averages. The Newark, New Jersey school district spends about $13,000 per student—a tuition in the range of the most elite private schools—yet conditions remained so abysmal that a few years ago the state was forced to take over control of the school district. Administration often siphons off fifty cents of every dollar earmarked for urban education—a factor that accounts in no small measure for the fact that inner-city private schools frequently outperform public schools at a fraction of the cost.

Further, three decades of racial balancing through mandatory student transfers and other forms of social engineering has not improved student achievement. Instead, it has produced mass white flight that has led to even more racially homogenous schools and sapped urban school districts of their middle-class base.[13] In fact, public schools themselves have undermined the common school ideal, not only in their racial and economic isolation but in their violent environments and in their failure to transmit shared American values. In stark contrast, as Sol Stern found in a recent study of inner-city Catholic schools, "Catholic schools have remained committed to the ideal that minority children can share in, and master, our civilization's intellectual and spiritual heritage. Indeed, Catholic schools are among the last bastions in American education of the idea of a common civic culture."[14]

The public school establishment's latest line is that we know what works—just give us the time and resources to do it. Of course, the response is that today's children don't have time to wait—nor should they be held hostage while the system responds. Even more to the point, if the people currently in charge know what to do, why don't they do it? Education analyst Chester E. Finn, Jr. offers five reasons why much-trumpeted public school reform fads often disappear without a trace: (1) the system does not reward risk-taking; (2) the system resists oversight from elected officials and the public; (3) the system is unaccountable for failure; (4) the system spends too little of its resources in the classroom; and (5) the consumers of education are no match for the system.[15] The third factor—accountability—is especially noteworthy, because it is usually the canard raised by public school advocates against private school choice: private schools aren't accountable. But private schools shut down if they don't produce the results that parents demand. Public schools, by contrast, almost never shut down, and defective teachers and administrators rarely lose their jobs. Public education is one of the few enterprises (the post office is another that comes to mind) that answers claims of inadequacy by demanding that consumers pay more for its services.

Nor is public school "choice" remotely sufficient to solve the urban education crisis. There simply aren't enough good public schools, particularly in the inner cities. In Chicago, for instance, more than half the city's public high schools rank in the *bottom 1 percent* nationally in academic performance. And without accountability—without funds and jobs at stake if the schools fail—or the flexibility to improve, public school choice merely will reshuffle students among public schools, with those who have the greatest influence finding their way into the best schools.[16]

The reality is that we know how to educate children from poor economic and family backgrounds. Pockets of high performance exist within the inner-city public school system. My former colleague, Nina Shokraii, who now is an education policy analyst for the Heritage Foundation, has profiled public education success stories. Rafe Esquith, for instance, teaches fifth and sixth grades of mostly poor Hispanic children at Hobart Elementary School in Los Angeles. By requiring them to read Shakespeare and perform difficult math equations—and by extending classroom hours to early mornings, late evenings, and weekends—Esquith has motivated and equipped his fifth-graders to score in the 98th percentile on mathematics and the 92nd in English in the Comprehensive Test of Basic Skills. As Shokraii explains, "Esquith's secret—which seems to be well kept from most of the education establishment—is his conviction that poor, inner-city kids can learn, and that the keys to educational success are high standards and hard work."[17]

But many of the success stories come from private schools. In cities throughout America, community private schools—many of them Catholic but others that are nonsectarian, Christian, or Islamic—toil with quiet success for economically disadvantaged children in poor neighborhoods. The schools operate on small budgets, charge little tuition, and demand substantial parental involvement—and they work. In Chicago's high-poverty Kenwood-Oakland Neighborhood, Holy Angels School's motto is "Where Proud Black Youngsters Produce and Achieve." The school serves 1,256 students, all of them black and poor, and charges only $40 to $45 per month tuition. "I feel like I'm in a war zone," the school's principal, Sister Helen Struder, says of the school's surroundings. But the children thrive. By stressing a basic curriculum, strict discipline, and high academic expectation, the school dramatically outpaces neighboring public schools in academic performance.[18]

I remember vividly my first visit to Holy Angels several years ago. Two students toured me around the school—a special privilege reserved for eighth graders. I stepped inside a kindergarten classroom and all at once forty or so beaming little faces wearing impish grins flashed in my direction. The children all wore school uniforms and had their hands folded on their desks; and aside from an occasional giggle, the children were quiet. Something seemed unusual about the classroom, and I realized there was no teacher present: she had stepped out for a moment, and those children were exercising self-discipline. It was wonderful. Even better were their faces, filled with hope and self-confidence. I remember thinking to myself: regardless of the challenges they face, those little kids are going somewhere.

That experience has replicated itself over and again as I've visited private inner-city schools around the country—schools like Messmer High School, Urban Day School, and Harambee in Milwaukee; the Hope Academies, St. Adalbert, and the Islamic School of the Oasis in Cleveland; Marcus Garvey School in south-central Los Angeles. There I have seen safe, orderly schools where positive values are imparted. I have seen committed parents, teachers, and administrators with control over the schools and classrooms making a difference in children's lives. I have seen children who display a strong sense of pride—not because they are taught empty self-esteem, but because they earn it. In fact, visiting the schools and

seeing how well the children are doing is one of my favorite parts of my
job, and it fuels me both with optimism and a keen sense of urgency.

Milwaukee's Messmer High School is a classic example. Like most successful inner-city schools, it is run by a strong principal—in this case,
Brother Bob Smith. His credo is *no excuses.* "We won't allow kids to perform poorly because they are poor, black, or from [one-parent] homes
and have often suffered years of neglect," he declares. Messmer's 320 students are 65 percent black and 10 percent Hispanic. In 1995, forty of the
school's fifty-two juniors taking the PSAT scored in the top 30th percentile
nationally. The school boasts a 98 percent graduation rate and 80 percent
go on to college—all achieved at a fraction of the cost of the Milwaukee
Public Schools.[19] (Unfortunately, because Messmer is an independent
Catholic school, it is presently excluded from the choice program,
although many of its students receive privately funded scholarships from a
community group, Partners Advancing Values in Education (PAVE).)

The cumulative effects of such private school efforts are impressive.
Echoing similarly positive findings from the 1980s,[20] University of
Chicago economist Derek Neal found recently that although Catholic
schools produce negligible academic effects for suburban and white
students, they strongly improve educational outcomes for urban minority children.[21] Holding other factors constant, Neal found that the odds
for high school graduation for urban black and Hispanic children
increase from 62 percent to at least 88 percent in Catholic schools. In
turn, he found that the likelihood of college graduation is tripled for
urban minority children who attend Catholic high schools. Not surprisingly, those gains translate into substantially higher wages in the
labor market. Neal concludes bluntly, "Urban minorities receive significant benefits from Catholic schooling because their public school
alternatives are substantially worse than those of whites or other minorities who live in rural or suburban areas."[22]

The superb track record of Catholic schools in educating poor
minority students manifested itself vividly in a 1995 challenge to New
York City officials from Cardinal John J. O'Connor: send us the lowest-
performing 5 percent of public school students and we guarantee they will
succeed. Both the Rand Corporation and the New York State Department
of Education have compared the record of New York City public and

Catholic schools in educating minority children from low-income families, and found substantially greater achievement in the Catholic schools.[23]

A New York philanthropist, Charles Benenson, funded the "I Have a Dream" program for public school students in the South Bronx, providing college tuition for students who graduate. Disappointed with the results, he started paying tuition for eighth-graders who wanted to attend Catholic schools. The results: out of thirty-eight students who stayed in public schools, only two made it to college; of twenty-two who attended Catholic schools, only two *didn't*. "They were the same kids from the same families and the same housing projects," reports Benenson. "In fact, sometimes one child went to a public school and a sibling went to Catholic school. We even gave money to the public-school kids for tutoring and after-school programs. It's just that the Catholic schools worked, and the others didn't."[24]

So the question presents itself: why are urban public schools so shockingly bad, when urban private schools and suburban public schools tend to do a decent job? That question was definitively addressed in a path-breaking Brookings Institution study by John E. Chubb and Terry M. Moe. They found that although student ability and parental background are important factors in student achievement, school organization also plays a substantial role. Specifically, they determined that over a four-year high school experience, effectively organized schools "increase the achievement of [their] students by more than one full year" over ineffectively organized schools.[25] The key difference is the degree of school autonomy. Chubb and Moe found that urban public schools are characterized by massive bureaucracies which make it difficult for teachers to teach, for parents to exercise influence, or for reform to take hold. Moreover, urban public schools are extremely susceptible to political manipulation by special interest groups, particularly teacher unions. Because many of their students are from poor families, the schools have a captive consumer base, so the school system has a greater incentive to satisfy the politicians who control their budgets than to satisfy parents. More affluent suburban families, by contrast, can exercise greater influence over their schools because they can move or send their children to private schools if they are dissatisfied with public schools. Private schools have the greatest incentive to satisfy parents, for their survival depends on satisfied customers. The private schools in low-income neighborhoods therefore tend to possess a keen sense of mission, offer an efficient product at low prices, and insist on parental involvement. Chubb and Moe concluded that greater parental choice is necessary for low-income parents to obtain the leverage to improve their children's education and to act as a prod to make public schools more efficient.

Making good on the promise of equal educational opportunities requires immediate and systemic institutional change, and fast. The experiences I have recounted suggest that we need what I call the two C's and three D's: choice, competition, deregulation, decentralization, and depoliticization. I sketch methods to achieve those goals below.

PARENTAL CHOICE

As revolutions go, the school choice revolution's beginnings were inauspicious. The movement's Lexington and Concord was Milwaukee, where in spring 1990 the nation's first low-income school choice program was enacted.

The program's initial provisions were modest, allowing up to one thousand low-income children who were enrolled in the Milwaukee Public Schools to use the state contribution to their education (about $2,500 per student) as full payment of tuition in participating nonsectarian private schools. But the program's enactment truly was the shot heard round the world.

Or at least a shot fired across the bow of the Wisconsin Education Association. Given such a modest program—involving a relative handful of children (only 1 percent of those enrolled in the Milwaukee Public Schools) and a fraction (about 40 percent) of per-pupil expenditures—one might expect an equally modest, if not even cautiously supportive, reaction. Particularly so given the abysmal performance of the Milwaukee Public Schools: the overall dropout rate was about 50 percent—and *85 percent* for children from families on public assistance—and the average grade-point for graduating black students was 1.5, or "D." By contrast, the graduation rate for inner-city private schools with predominantly minority populations was over 90 percent. Dr. Howard Fuller, who served from 1991–95 as MPS superintendent, recounts that "[f]or a significant number of kids, particularly poor

African-American kids, . . . we had a system that was failing."[26] Dr.
Fuller supported the original choice program:

> I felt that it was in the best interest of poor parents for them
> to have the capacity to affect what happens to their kids. I feel
> that people who have money in America already have that option.
> I believe that when you get to a situation where dollars follow stu-
> dents, that has a certain impact on the system. I always felt that
> the issue was not how do you protect the system, but how do you
> enhance learning opportunities for families. And I felt that the
> Choice Program . . . should be a part of the mix.[27]

But Fuller's was the lonely voice of reason within the Wisconsin
education establishment. It was as if an atomic bomb had exploded in
Milwaukee. The union responded with hysteria and shrill predictions
of doom. The anti-choice forces launched a two-front attack against
the choice program: first, the union (with the Milwaukee branch of
the NAACP shilling as the lead plaintiff) filed a lawsuit challenging
the program's constitutionality; second, Wisconsin Superintendent of
Public Instruction Herbert Grover imposed a blizzard of regulations on
the private schools, threatening to sentence the program to death by
bureaucratic strangulation.

The parents and children were obliged to fight back, defending the
program in court and challenging the legality of the regulations. We had
to succeed on both fronts in order for the program to commence on
schedule in September 1990.

As the lawyer representing the parents and children, I learned a
great deal about David versus Goliath tactics from the program's main
sponsor, State Rep. Annette "Polly" Williams, a former welfare recipient, mother of four, and a Democrat. Williams was accustomed to
fighting powerful forces. She had discovered that roughly half of the
employees of the Milwaukee Public Schools send their own children to
private schools. "It's funny," she told me, "that they think the public
schools are good enough for *our* kids, but not for *theirs*." So Williams
announced she would introduce a bill that would require school
employees, as a condition of employment, to send their children to

public schools. The reaction was outrage—and death threats on Polly Williams' answering machine.

Why the hysterical reaction to such a modest experiment? Two reasons. First, the program marked a transfer of *power* over basic educational choices from bureaucrats to low-income parents, who have the greatest stake in their children's education. Second, for the first time in American history, the program created *competition* for low-income children and the dollars they now commanded. Previously, those children had no place to go other than the public schools to which they were assigned, no matter how abysmal. Now, they were able to walk out the schoolhouse doors—and more important, to take a share of their funds with them. Finally, low-income parents had gained a measure of the clout routinely wielded by higher-income and suburban parents. And the education bureaucrats couldn't stand it.

In August 1990, after a grueling hearing packed with parents and children wearing "School Choice" buttons, Dane County Circuit Judge Susan Steingass upheld the program and struck down the most offensive regulations. The litigation would last two more years, with the Court of Appeals striking down the program, then a 4–3 majority of the Wisconsin Supreme Court upholding the program in spring 1992. "The Wisconsin legislature . . . has attempted to throw a life preserver to those Milwaukee children caught in the cruel riptide of a school system floundering upon the shoals of poverty, status-quo thinking, and despair," declared Justice Louis Ceci. "Let's give choice a chance!"[28]

But by the time of the 1992 Wisconsin Supreme Court ruling, the seminal battle had already been won: on the day that school started in September 1990 and several hundred economically disadvantaged children crossed the threshold to a brighter future, the world had changed and there was no going back. The idea of school choice had taken root, and the apocalyptic predictions by anti-choice activists finally could be put to the test.

From the start, the Milwaukee program endured serious constraints that limited its potential. The program initially was limited to one thousand children (though the number was soon raised to fifteen hundred). Only nonsectarian schools could participate, and they were unable to make enough seats available for all the children who wanted them. And schools could accept only half (later 65 percent) of their students from the choice program, inhibiting new schools from opening to meet the demand.

Moreover, early reports on the program's performance were only marginally positive. The state's official researcher, Professor John Witte, was hand-picked by Superintendent Grover and given exclusive access to student achievement data. Each year Witte released a report, and each year the results were the same: parents were highly satisfied with the program and they were active in the schools—but the students demonstrated no academic gains. The reports seemed to defy a basic tenet of educational research, namely that parental involvement strongly correlates with academic success.[29] But no one could check Witte's findings, because he refused to release the data.

Still, the program proved popular: the *Milwaukee Community Journal*, the city's largest African-American newspaper, found that 90 percent of the Milwaukee's blacks supported the program. Meanwhile, the state auditor found that the children in the program were even poorer than the children left behind in the public schools[30]—precisely opposite the "cream-skimming" predicted by choice opponents.

After five years of experience with the program, education reform activists mobilized to expand the program. The coalition behind expansion was remarkable: thousands of low-income inner-city parents banded together to form Parents for School Choice, and they were backed by the Metropolitan Milwaukee Chamber of Commerce, Republican Governor Tommy Thompson, and Democratic Mayor John Norquist. Their efforts paid off in spring 1995 when a bipartisan majority of the legislature voted to expand the program in three major ways: increasing the number of eligible children ten-fold to fifteen thousand; allowing religious schools to participate; and lifting the cap on the percentage of children schools could enroll from the program. By September 1995, more than one hundred of Milwaukee's 120 private schools had agreed to participate, and several thousand children had applied.

But the Wisconsin Education Association, the NAACP, and the American Civil Liberties Union again went to court, arguing among other things that the program constituted an establishment of religion in violation of the United States and Wisconsin Constitutions. On the eve of the school year, the Wisconsin Supreme Court issued an injunction

against the program's expansion; and as of publication time, the litigation persists. A massive outpouring of community financial support
from the Bradley Foundation, PAVE, and thousands of others kept
most of the children in their chosen schools during the litigation.

But as the battle waged in the courtroom, it was being won in the
court of public opinion. In the midst of the litigation, a new study on
student performance in the choice program was released by Harvard
Professor Paul Peterson, who had managed after a protracted battle to
pry loose the data previously monopolized by John Witte. It turns out
that Witte had compared performance of students in the choice program with a subset of MPS schoolchildren, essentially comparing
apples to oranges—and overlooking the obvious comparison group:
children who had applied for the program but were turned away by
random selection. Peterson compared kids who were accepted with
those who applied but were denied and remained in MPS, and found
results quite different than Witte. Over the first two years in the
choice program, performance between the two groups differed little.
But in the third year, test scores for choice program students improved
in both reading and mathematics, and in the fourth year they soared. In
sum, for minority students in the choice program for four years, the gap
between minority and nonminority test scores closed by between
one-third to one-half, an absolutely stupendous gain.[31]

Though the Peterson study's findings were challenged by Witte and
others, they were no surprise to people involved in the program. Zakiya
Courtney, director of Parents for School Choice, testified that

> I was glad to see . . . a study that reflected what many of us
> who have been working directly with the families and the children
> all along knew. And that is that parental satisfaction does make a
> difference; and that oftentimes you may not see those high
> achievement scores in the beginning, but if you give those chil-
> dren the opportunity to stay and work in the program, that you
> do see those differences.[32]

The program has positive ramifications not only for the children
involved, but for those left behind in the public schools. Howard Fuller,

who resigned as MPS superintendent in 1995 over the slow pace of reform, championed the choice program's expansion because the original program was too small to trigger systemic change in the public schools. "I wanted it to have an impact," he explains, "because I wanted to have a different discussion about what we were going to do to make sure that parents wanted to keep their kids in our school district."[33] At an evidentiary hearing on August 15, 1996, Fuller testified on the likely effect of the expanded program:

> I think that what it will bring into play would be, in addition to the existing schools, there will be new schools out there that will come into being that will find their niche to begin to reach kids that we are not currently reaching or that we're losing. I think it will begin to give poor parents some capacity to have leverage over this entire discussion. And the reason they will have leverage is because they will begin to have control over resources, the same type of control over resources that people with money have. . . . You begin to create a synergism for change that I think is key, if the system is going to be changed, so that we . . . save these kids that we're losing each and every day.[34]

Fuller's successor as MPS superintendent, Robert Jasna, grudgingly agreed that choice has been a catalyst for positive public school reform. Testifying for the choice opponents, Jasna pointed to several reforms adopted by MPS in recent years, including adopting tougher standards, placing more control of funds in the hands of school principals, increasing parental involvement, closing failing schools, and creating specialty and charter schools. (Not surprisingly, Jasna's efforts to close failing schools and to open charter schools were blocked in court by the same teachers' union that challenged the choice program.) When I cross-examined Jasna, he acknowledged that the choice program has prompted positive reforms. "It does make people change," he conceded.[35]

The strongest support for the program comes, not surprisingly, from the parents themselves. Pilar Gonzalez wasn't able to afford private school tuition, though she wanted an alternative for her children, nine-year-old Andres, who was having trouble because of a partial hearing loss; and seven-year-old Bianca, whose behavior sometimes caused problems. She obtained a PAVE half-tuition scholarship to send the children to St. Lawrence, a Catholic elementary school, and both children have blossomed. But without the choice program, the Gonzalez family may not be able to afford to keep them there. "I know I'd make every sacrifice possible before I allowed them to go back," Pilar Gonzalez says determinedly.[36]

Valerie Johnson and her husband have struggled to put five children through Catholic school, even though they are Pentecostals. Ms. Johnson testified about the sacrifices that has required, and the reasons: "[W]e don't have a car. We just can't afford to get one and pay the insurance. We don't eat a lot of fast food. We don't take family vacations. But we felt all these things were really important to sacrifice to help give our children the best education possible.[37]

The Johnsons' investment is paying off: their eldest child was accepted to Xavier University in New Orleans. But the college expenses have placed even greater strain on their family, so they were excited when the choice program was expanded to include religious schools. Ms. Johnson expressed widespread community sentiment:

> I said Wow, finally the system cares. I mean, I'm not going to be out here sacrificing all by myself anymore; the system is going to help. And so I was really elated. And then when I realized that it was halted, I had a real sense of feeling that the system don't care that I'm a parent left out here on my own because I don't have the financial means; that they didn't care about that. That my children are not worthy enough to have a better education because I didn't have that choice. And I was very frustrated. There were many letters that I wrote, but didn't send, because it was out of anger and you can't accomplish anything in anger. But I was very, very disappointed.[38]

As Milwaukee was busy fighting against entrenched interests to build on the success of its school choice program, a second program was launched in Cleveland. If anything, the Cleveland public schools were even worse than Milwaukee's; so bad that in 1995, the district became the largest in the United States to have its governance transferred to the state by federal court order.

Councilwoman Fannie Lewis, who represents the Hough neighborhood of Cleveland—which still bears the scars of devastating riots three decades ago—was a prime catalyst for school choice. She organized several buses of parents to lobby legislators in Columbus in support of a scholarship program sponsored by Governor George Voinovich. Their efforts paid off in 1995 with the enactment of a program that provides two thousand scholarships to low-income children to cover 90 percent of private school tuition, which is capped at $2,500. Remarks Councilwoman Lewis, "Most parents in Hough want the same thing as parents anywhere else: good schools in their own communities. This scholarship program is the start of making that possibility a reality for families who lack alternatives right now."[39]

As in Milwaukee, the leviathan fought back. Rival teacher unions—the National Education Association and the American Federation of Teachers—joined forces with the ACLU, People for the American Way, and other groups to challenge the program in court. Once again, my colleagues and I joined the program's defense on behalf of parents and children. More than one hundred parents and children traveled with us to Columbus on a bus caravan on the eve of the trial court argument to demonstrate in favor of school choice. We won the opening round, with the result that in September 1996, the first low-income children in America were able to use a share of their education funds not only in private nonsectarian schools, but also religious ones.

One parent, Jennifer Kinsey, chose to use a scholarship to send her little girl, Jermaine, to kindergarten at Metro Catholic after visiting the school. "In the classes I visited the kids were calm, quiet, and busy," in stark contrast to the Cleveland Public Schools, Ms. Kinsey attests. "The classrooms were bright and cheery, full of pictures drawn by the children. You could tell the children enjoyed learning and that the teachers enjoyed teaching."

Jennifer Kinsey joined the program's legal defense, explaining that

If the Scholarship Program is struck down I will be devastated. Jermaine will be very disappointed, too. When she found out she got the scholarship, she was so happy she went through her daycare center bragging about it for days. She is just so excited to have this chance. It would be a travesty to tell these kids they cannot have this chance to get ahead. This program gave me a choice for my children—I don't want it taken away.[40]

As the inner-city public schools grow worse despite ever-growing subsidies and myriad "reforms"—and as the promise of choice grows more evident—the nontraditional coalition behind choice has grown beyond the alliance between conservative Republicans and low-income minorities that produced the Milwaukee program. It now receives strong support from moderate Republicans such as Governors George Voinovich, Arne Carlson, and Pete Wilson; progressive Democrats such as Milwaukee Mayor John Norquist, Puerto Rico Governor Pedro Rossello, and former Clinton White House policy advisor William Galston; and former Rep. Floyd Flake (D-NY). In 1997, Arizona joined the ranks of school choice states by enacting a $500 tax credit for contributions to private scholarship funds; and other states and localities around the nation appear poised to adopt school choice in one form or another.

Some doubt the potential for school choice, observing correctly that existing private schools are too few to absorb large numbers of low-income children. But supply is not finite if demand grows. Akron industrialist David Brennan established two nonsectarian Hope Academies in the first year of the Cleveland scholarship program. Several new private schools were set to open in Milwaukee when the program's expansion was enjoined. The greatest potential for new schools is in churches, whose Sunday school classrooms are often unused during weekdays. At a meeting of about 150 black ministers at the Heritage Foundation several years ago, I asked how many operated elementary schools. About one-quarter raised their hands. When I asked how many would open schools if children had vouchers, fully half raised their hands.

In any event, most parents probably will remain with the public schools if their children are doing well there. Choice will give even those parents greater leverage because for the first time they will have the choice to leave. Our goal for public schools should be a system that exists not because parents have no other choice, but one that thrives because families choose to send their children there.

Some libertarians oppose school choice because they worry, legitimately, that it will expose private schools to greater regulations. So far, that fear has not been realized: we successfully beat back regulations in Milwaukee; and a voucher program in certain rural school districts has existed in Vermont for more than a century without any imposition of private school regulations. Indeed, school choice so far seems to have the opposite effect: creating pressure to *deregulate* gives public schools greater autonomy, as in Milwaukee. But even if the worst-case scenario came true, private schools always can opt out of the programs and maintain complete independence. The status quo is too intolerable to preserve in the face of hypothetical concerns.

Public opinion seems highly amenable to school choice. The Hoover Institution's Terry M. Moe has conducted extensive polling on the issue.[41] Remarkably, about two-thirds of all respondents—including 82 percent of poor inner-city respondents—had never heard anything about school vouchers. Described as a system where children receive state grants that they may use in private or parochial schools, in addition to their choice to attend public schools, the idea was favored by a substantial majority of all respondents. Public school parents favored or strongly favored the idea by a margin of 71 to 21 percent over those who strongly or somewhat opposed it. Support was strongest among the inner-city poor, who backed school choice by 84 in favor to only 9 percent opposed. Most respondents—including the inner-city poor—favored a statewide choice system over one limited to low-income families. A large majority of respondents believed that competition would help rather than hurt public schools; and by a margin of better than 7 to 1 the respondents opined that religious schools should be included among the range of options.

Those statistics demonstrate the political potential for parental choice: if supporters have a chance to make their case, they will find a receptive public. Furthermore, the strongest supporters are those who stand to benefit most: the inner-city poor.

School choice is not a panacea, but it is a prerequisite to delivering on the promise of equal educational opportunities. Alone among school reforms, it promises to move children out of failing schools and into good schools, and to do so *today*—not ten years from now, not another wasted billion dollars from now, but *now*. And alone it creates a competitive incentive for public schools to shake off years of lethargy and to return to their core mission.

Having seen parental choice work its not-so-mysterious magic in Milwaukee and Cleveland, I favor the broadest possible school choice programs—including religious schools among the range of options—with the greatest resources targeted to low-income youngsters. I also support choice as part of a broader program of public school reform, unshackling public schools to respond effectively to the new competitive reality. But even without such additional steps—for public school reform likely will follow adoption of school choice programs in any event—I believe school choice is the most vitally important reform in America today. If we could do only one thing to improve the prospects for economically disadvantaged families, school choice should be the first priority.

For many of the children who benefit from it, choice literally will make the difference between life and death. For millions of others, it can mean for the first time something approaching equal educational opportunities, at long last helping to fulfill America's most important promise. For too often, "the present school system is the vehicle that puts us on welfare, in prison, and leaves us illiterate," says Anyam Palmer, principal of Marcus Garvey School in south-central Los Angeles. "School choice is the only way out of this vicious cycle."[42]

CHARTER SCHOOLS

Cordia Booth has taught in the Denver Public Schools for twenty-two years. Despite the best efforts of Booth and other public school teachers, she despairs over the fate of poor and minority youngsters. "Every year it is worse. Test scores are worse; dropout rates are worse," she laments. "After hearing that for all those years, the only way to accept it and move on is to say that minority kids simply cannot achieve. I can't do that. I can't turn my back on these kids."[43]

So Booth and other teachers and parents decided to do something nearly unprecedented: they decided to break the mold and start their own public school. Enabled by Colorado's charter school law, Booth

secured permission to open the Thurgood Marshall Charter Middle
School. The school would have no principal, just thirteen teachers
helping parents run the school. It would have a longer school day and
a curriculum centered on five basic subjects: English, math, science,
social studies, and Spanish. Even before it opened its doors, the school
attracted a waiting list of thirteen students.

Radical? Hardly, by any real-world definition of the term. But
unsettling enough to the education establishment to precipitate a major
battle, including a lawsuit filed by the Denver Board of Education challenging the new school's charter. More restrictive than many other
states, Colorado's charter school law requires consent from the local
school board to start a new school. Though by 1997 there were twenty-
seven charter schools operating statewide, the Denver school board had
approved only three out of fifteen applicants. This in a school district
that has lost more than forty-five thousand white students since forced
busing was ordered thirty years ago, and where students score in the
35th percentile in reading and math on standardized tests.

Cordia Booth is determined to fight for her school. "This district
needs something like this desperately," she urges. "Otherwise it will
continue to be a highly centralized bureaucracy that is out of touch."

Charter schools are the *perestroika* to school choice's *glasnost*: an
education reform halfway house, allowing for the creation of new public
schools that enjoy greater autonomy. As of 1997, twenty-five states and
the District of Columbia had adopted charter school laws, including six
new jurisdictions in 1996.[44] According to the Center for Education
Reform (CER), the programs have yielded 480 schools serving over
105,000 students.[45]

But not all charter school programs are alike. The one characteristic
common to all charter schools is that they are public schools that are
exempted from some state regulations. As Chester E. Finn, Jr. and
Diane Ravitch describe charter schools:

> Some were regular public schools that seceded—their coun-
> terparts in England are called "opt-out" schools and became
> self-governing. Others are new schools started by teachers, par-
> ents, private firms, universities, girls' clubs and an astonishing

array of other organizations. They are generally free to budget their own resources, select their own teachers, schedule their time and create their own curriculum. They charge no tuition, have no admissions requirements, and are attended only by students whose families choose them.[46]

Charter schools gain independence by promising to achieve certain results. The charters and funding are granted by state or local educational authorities, usually for five years. If the promised results are achieved, the charter is renewed; if not, the school closes. "What makes charter schools so promising an education reform strategy," observes Finn in a recent analysis co-authored with Bruno V. Manno and Louann A. Bierlein, "is that they are accountable for results rather than adherence to rules"[47]—precisely the opposite of ordinary public schools.

But from that common point the programs vary dramatically in the degree of autonomy. For that reason, three states—California, Arizona, and Michigan—account for about three-fourths of all charter schools and total charter enrollment. By contrast, nine states—Arkansas, Connecticut, Kansas, New Hampshire, New Jersey, North Carolina, Rhode Island, South Carolina, and Wyoming—have charter school laws on the books, but as of November 1996 not a single charter school had opened in those states.

The divergent results are explained by the diametrically opposite objectives served in different states by charter school legislation: either as a serious education reform; or as a means to stave off reform by pretending to create autonomy but in reality maintaining bureaucratic control. As Finn and Ravitch explain, "Some of these laws were supported by people who actually oppose charter schools on principle and decided that the best way to defuse support for the idea was to promote a bill that pretended to create them."[48]

The Center for Education Reform has prepared a rating system to assess the efficacy of charter school laws, evaluating them on ten factors:[49]

- *Numbers: how many are permitted?*
- *Multiple chartering authorities/appeals:* how many entities have authority to issue charters?

- *Variety of applicants:* how flexible is the law in terms of the individuals and entities who may start charter schools?
- *New starts:* does the law allow creation of new schools as well as conversion of existing public schools?
- *Local support requirement:* do charter schools require formal demonstration of support?
- *Automatic waivers of regulations?*
- *Legal autonomy?*
- *Full funding:* are charter schools guaranteed full per-pupil funding?
- *Budget autonomy?*
- *Collective bargaining:* are charter schools exempted from ordinary collective bargaining requirements?

On a possible eleven-point range (the second factor, multiple chartering authorities and appeals, was accorded two points), CER ranked each of the twenty-six jurisdictions on the efficacy of their charter school laws (point totals in parentheses):

1. Arizona (11)
2. District of Columbia (10.5)
3. Michigan (10)
4. Delaware (9.5)
5. North Carolina (9)
6. Florida (9)
7. Massachusetts (8.5)
8. South Carolina (8.5)
9. Illinois (8.5)
10. Minnesota (8)
11. New Hampshire (8)
12. New Jersey (8)
13. California (7.5)
14. Texas (7)
15. Colorado (7)
16. Louisiana (7)
17. Connecticut (7)

18. Wisconsin (6)
19. Alaska (4.5)
20. Rhode Island (4)
21. Wyoming (4)
22. Kansas (3)
23. New Mexico (2.5)
24. Hawaii (2.5)
25. Georgia (2)
26. Arkansas (1.5)

(In 1997, Ohio passed wide-ranging charter school legislation and New Jersey liberalized its charter school laws.)

The widely divergent results illustrate the vast range of charter school options; not surprisingly, the states with "strong" charter school laws have experienced substantial dynamism within their education systems; while those (like Arkansas) with "weak" laws have maintained the status quo.[50]

Among existing charter programs, Arizona's and Michigan's generally are acknowledged as the most far-reaching. "Given the strength of the political opposition, Michigan's charter school story is one to be viewed with awe," report Finn, Manno, and Bierlein in their 1996 study *Charter Schools in Action: What Have We Learned?* That the charter program exists at all is attributable to the vision, determination, and political acumen of Governor John Engler. After the initial law was declared unconstitutional by the Michigan Supreme Court in 1993, the legislature enacted a revised version less than a month later.[51] The law allows any individual or group to start a charter school with approval from one of four entities: local school boards, intermediate school district boards, community college boards, or state public university boards. The cap on charters rises each year, to 150 after 1998. Except for charter schools approved by local boards of education, the schools are independent legal entities and are exempted from collective bargaining and teacher tenure laws. The schools receive the prevailing local per-pupil expenditure, not to exceed $5,500 (adjusted for inflation from 1994–95 dollars). By 1997, seventy-three charter schools were open, enrolling twelve thousand students.

Two Afrocentric schools in Michigan, Sankofa Shule in Lansing and Aisha Shule in Detroit, attest to the program's flexibility. Sankofa was started as a charter school by teachers and parents who were frustrated over the local district's bureaucracy. The school stresses such values as truth, justice, and righteousness, and emphasizes educational basics. "I had two students who were in special education" in the public schools, remarks Freya Rivers, Sankofa's founder, principal, and language-arts teacher. "They couldn't even write their names or recognize any words." That has changed. "I use the same methods to teach them that I use with other students," Rivers says. "Now both of them are writing sentences."[52]

Aisha Shule started twenty years ago as a private school. Having transitioned into a charter school, Aisha has expanded its enrollment from 90 to 210. "There were a lot of people who always wanted to put their children in our school but couldn't afford it," explains founder Imani Humphrey. The school's results are impressive: last year, while only 22 percent of Detroit public school seventh-graders scored satisfactory in reading and math, 71 percent of Aisha's seventh-graders scored satisfactory in reading and 64 percent in math. Two parents, Linda and Travis Sherer, mortgaged their home to obtain funds to lease Aisha's building. "We decided to help launch the school and send our six-year-old son, Jason, to it because of the individualized instruction," says Linda Sherer. "I've seen what happens to young black kids in the Michigan criminal justice system. We decided that either we would pay up front and give our boy the opportunity to get a good foundation, or suffer the consequences."

Sankofa Shule has pioneered a new technique to counteract unruly students: instead of suspending the children from school, they suspend the parent from work, requiring the parent to attend school with the child and help work out the problem. "So far we haven't had one parent who hasn't shown up, or one child who has continued to act up," says Freya Rivers. If only other public schools were given the power to effectively deal with disciplinary problems!

Arizona's charter school law is even more sweeping than Michigan's. The law was pioneered by the creative and dynamic State Superintendent of Public Instruction, Lisa Graham Keegan, who as a state legislator in 1994 came within a few votes of enacting a school choice program. At the end she agreed to a compromise—the nation's most flexible and far-reaching charter school law—and then won election as the statewide official responsible for implementing it.

Features of the program include multiple chartering authorities, a generous and expanding cap on the number of charter schools, full per-pupil operating funds, flexibility in who is eligible to start charter schools (including for-profit corporations), ownership of school assets, light regulatory oversight, and long-term (fifteen-year) charters. As *Charter Schools in Action* reports, the "favorable climate has fostered a remarkably diverse array of charter schools," such an Indian reservation school, a Waldorf-style school started out of a private preschool, a school begun as a boys' and girls' club, a school created by a Hispanic community development corporation, and a multi-site school for dropouts and ex-offenders.[53] By 1997, there were 164 charter schools enrolling about seventeen thousand students—fully 2 percent of all Arizona students.[54] The charter schools are primarily serving students who are not faring well in traditional public school environments. "I can't think of a single charter school that is filled with overachievers," says John Kafritz, chief executive officer of the Arizona Charter Schools Association. "They are all getting students with academic problems, even the ones who billed themselves as wanting to attract the best and the brightest."[55] The Arizona experience mirrors national charter school statistics: *Charter Schools in Action* found that 49 percent of charter school students are black or Hispanic.[56]

Charter schools are not without problems. Several have closed due to mismanagement. But that is the point. "It's a sign of strength that charters work because when one fails we don't keep it on life support," says Chester Finn. "Please tell me how many regular schools have been closed for cause."[57]

Not surprisingly, even though they give teachers greater autonomy, the unions have resorted to legal challenges when they haven't succeeded in blocking meaningful charter school programs in the legislature. One Michigan teacher describes it:

> As a 25-year public school veteran and former union member, I was shocked at MEA's all-out attack on our charter school law. They were very effective in killing our initial law and almost shut-

ting down this charter school. They obviously have lost any focus they might have had on teaching and learning.[58]

That teacher shouldn't be surprised: with the extensive and well-funded arsenal of special-interest litigation groups ready to deploy against any meaningful education reform, litigation has become a reliable measure of the potency of reform: if the reform program is not challenged in court, it shows that probably nothing significant was accomplished.

But as charter schools and other education reforms that empower parents take hold, the special interest groups will find their war of attrition a losing one. "The charter legislation has given us in the minority community the power to control and change schools, the power to take schools back after years of failure brought on by those who were well-intentioned but naive about integration and busing," says one community activist.[59] "We know that the union doesn't want to give up power," warns another. "But we also know that the union can continue to do what they've been doing only if we allow them to do it. And we've reached the point where we've said that we won't allow it anymore."[60]

THE INFRASTRUCTURE FOR REFORM: CHILD-CENTERED EDUCATION FUNDING

School choice, charter schools, and other promising education reforms all distill to a single key concept: what Arizona Superintendent of Education Lisa Graham Keegan calls "strapping education funding to the child's back."[61] After decades of focusing on supporting public schools as ends in themselves, we need to redefine the terms of the debate: the purpose of public education is not to serve the system, but to serve the children. The one-size-fits-all approach to education has failed. The conceptual breakthrough necessary to achieve true systemic reform is that we should fund students, not schools. Child-centered funding means choice, competition, fairness, and a system geared to meeting the needs of each individual child. Who provides that education—and where that education is delivered—is a concern secondary to the fact that education is taking place.

Those who support parental choice in private schools are often accused of abandoning public schools and pursuing means that are too radical. Ironically, the slow progress toward parental choice in fact may result from failing to be radical *enough*. Fundamental reform—change that will improve educational opportunities for all children—must encompass public as well as private schools. The vast potential of child-centered education funding for public schools lies in the fact that when funds are directed by parents to public schools, they stay in those schools. When funds are placed by parents at the disposal of principals and teachers—rather than allocated and absorbed by the bureaucracy—it will empower schools to improve and concentrate on providing quality education. Moreover, whereas school choice is sometimes a tough sell, the more-sweeping concept of child-centered education funding seems to strike a positive visceral chord in most people. It is the broad theme and infrastructure within which empowerment advocates should wrap their proposals for education reform.

That means abandoning the popular conservative mantra of "local autonomy." In practice, local autonomy means control of local school districts, which are government monopolies. As such, typically they resist reforms and impose layers of stifling bureaucracy upon the schools. Rejecting local autonomy does not mean federal or even state control, but rather greater power for parents, teachers, and principals. When parents direct state funds straight to the schools of their choice, school district bureaucracies and the special-interest groups that control them will be rendered largely obsolete.

Likewise, in the course of promoting systemic education reform—and necessarily fighting the education establishment—it is a mistake, both strategically and substantively, to make our message in any manner anti-teacher. Reforms ought to focus on giving teachers greater freedom to teach and on separating the interests of teachers from bureaucrats.[62]

Ultimately, we must regain the leadership role on education issues and forge nontraditional alliances to accomplish urgently needed systemic reform. Education reform should not mean greater federal control, increased funding for school bureaucrats, or greater homogeneity in educational techniques. It should mean empowerment of parents, teachers, and communities. It must mean those things, and we must accomplish them—soon—if we are to deliver on our nation's guarantee of equal educational opportunities.

ACTION PROPOSALS

1. *Child-centered education funding.* As the overarching education reform, we should refocus educational funding away from school systems to students, placing educational funding at the disposal of families to choose the most suitable education for their children. Families would be free to choose from public or private schools, or even nontraditional educational alternatives such as homeschooling or distance learning. Funding directed by parents to schools would be placed under that school's exclusive control, rather than funneled through school districts. The state's role would focus on ensuring that education takes place, rather than dictating how education is provided.

In addition to promoting choice and competition, this reform would also achieve the ultimate in educational funding equalization: every child will have the identical amount of funding from the state. The amount available can be calculated on the basis of per-pupil spending minus fixed costs of operation and capital expenditures. Until school systems no longer view education funding as an entitlement—and until school failure triggers real-world consequences—we will not have the accountable, consumer-driven public school system we need. Student-based funding would give parents, rather than politicians and special-interest groups, power over their children's education.

2. *Parental choice.* States and localities should adopt the broadest possible programs allowing children to choose private as well as public schools. School choice should be the empowerment movement's most urgent priority, for it offers the most immediate prospect for expanding educational opportunities for children who need them most desperately. As a remedial measure, choice could be targeted to economically disadvantaged youngsters, educationally at-risk students, and/or students attending poor-performing or dangerous schools. To allow the

greatest diversity of choices, religious schools should be included among the range of options; and to ensure autonomy, regulations of private schools should be minimal.

Prospects for choice depend ultimately on the resolution of ongoing legal challenges. Defenders of the status quo use not only the federal constitution but state constitutions to challenge school choice, and their litigation teams are well-funded and determined. We must make sure that parents and children are always well-represented in the courtroom and the court of public opinion. But while the legal battles continue, reform advocates should keep pressing for school choice: once conferred, freedom is hard to take away.

3. *Charter schools.* States should adopt strong charter school laws modeled on the Arizona and Michigan examples, or revise their existing charter laws to create greater flexibility and autonomy. Features of successful charter laws include a broad range of charter school sponsors (existing public schools, private schools, individuals, organizations, and for-profit corporations), multiple chartering agencies, full per-pupil funding, exemptions from bureaucratic edicts, and few regulations. Charter schools provide greater accountability because they can exist only if they attract students and achieve their educational objectives. They also provide greater flexibility and creativity to teachers and administrators.

4. *Privatized teacher-owned schools.* The concept of privatized teacher-owned schools (PTOS) combines two concepts that have improved efficiency in service delivery in other industries: privatization and employee stock-ownership plans. Essentially, PTOS would involve selling schools to teachers and administrators; in some cases allowing the use of teacher pension funds for investment capital. School districts would agree to allow public school students to choose PTOS and to take their per-pupil funds with them. Alternatively, school districts could contract directly with PTOS to provide educational services. PTOS expands upon the

charter school model by giving teachers an ownership stake in their schools. It also demonstrates that good teachers have nothing to lose—and much to gain—from a system of free choice.

5. *The three D's for public school governance.* In terms of traditional public school governance, reform should be guided by the three D's: deregulation, decentralization, and depoliticization. To the greatest possible degree, power over personnel, budget, curriculum, and school policies should be transferred to the school level. Indeed, schools should be given greater power over disciplinary policies, perhaps setting up test cases that will challenge past judicial precedents that removed a great deal of disciplinary power from school authorities. The more that public schools operate on principles of choice and contract rather than coercion, the greater flexibility the federal courts are likely to accord them.

6. *Empowering teachers and disempowering unions.* The greatest obstacle to any kind of meaningful education reform is teacher unions, which control and wield vast resources in the policy and legal arenas. Their interests are not always in accord with their members, and nearly always at odds with the purposes of public education. In addition to superb efforts by such groups as the Alexis de Tocqueville Institution and the Center for Education Reform to publicize the activities and objectives of the unions, pro-reform activists should take steps to neutralize union political power while at the same time pushing pro-teacher reforms.

In addition to charter schools and privatized teacher-owned schools, two proposals seem especially promising. First, groups like the Evergreen Freedom Foundation in Washington State have pioneered efforts to monitor union spending in elections (particularly initiatives concerning education), and to push initiatives and legislation to allow teachers to withdraw the portion of their dues allocated for political purposes—a right exercised by the vast majority of teachers where an opt-out is provided by law.

Another possible ballot or legislative measure would create a floor for the percentage of public school funding that must be spent in classrooms. The greatest growth in education spending over the past decade by far has taken place in administration rather than classroom spending—in some cases, fifty cents of every dollar is siphoned off by the bureaucracy before it reaches the classroom. A floor of perhaps 75 percent for classroom spending would translate into less bureaucracy, greater teacher autonomy, and perhaps even higher teacher salaries—all of which would separate teachers from administrators.

7. *Refocus affirmative action.* Race-based affirmative action has emphasized redistributing opportunities instead of increasing the number of people capable of competing on a level playing field.[63] As renowned civil libertarian Nat Hentoff has observed, the "basic concern has been with merely improving the statistics of black enrollment—without doing the hard, sometimes expensive work, of preparing youngsters of low-income families for college."[64]

We should abandon the race-and-redistribution approach in favor of one that increases human capital. As Nancy Hoffman urges, if we truly want diversity, "it is time to shift our emphasis . . . to the preparation of minority students for academic success."[65] One such program is MESA, a University of California program that targets low-income students and provides special classes to prepare them for study in engineering and science. James Taylor, the principal of Martin Luther King, Jr. Middle School in one of San Franscisco's poorest neighborhoods, stresses the importance of "just exposing them early enough to get on track for the right courses in high school and the right track to college. To make sure they are qualified, we have to start very, very early."[66] Applying this model on a larger scale, the University of California is targeting 450 underachieving schools and helping provide more college-prep courses, improve teacher preparation, and fund scholarships, all toward the goal of doubling the number of black and Hispanic students who can meet the strict admissions requirements of the state's elite postsecondary schools.[67]

Affirmative action that fails to address the underlying causes of racial disparities—or that fails to deliver its benefits to the truly disadvantaged—is a fraud. Everyone profits when more people have the tools to compete and to earn a share of the American Dream. That is what affirmative action should be about.

8. *Choice remedies in funding equity and desegregation lawsuits.* Despite their failure to substantially improve educational quality, funding equity and desegregation lawsuits remain a favorite tool in the left-wing legal arsenal. To the extent such efforts succeed (or to the extent they persist, as in the case of desegregation remedies, many of which are four decades old), reform advocates should promote the only true remedy: child-centered education funding and school choice. In the area of children who are entitled to assistance under the Individuals with Disabilities Education Act (IDEA), the U.S. Supreme Court has held repeatedly that where public school authorities default on their obligation to provide a "free appropriate education," the children are entitled to attend private schools at public expense.[68] Although we should not be eager to accept this model in its entirety—school districts are exposed to virtually open-ended financial liability—it does provide a precedent for an opt-out remedy that makes the child whole. Pro-reform advocates should seek to intervene on behalf of children whenever possible in funding equity and desegregation lawsuits to seek the proper remedy.

9. *Private scholarships.* Finally, businesses, foundations, and individuals should invest in private scholarship programs that have spread nationwide in recent years with the support of such pioneers as Golden Rule Insurance Company's J. Patrick Rooney, who launched the Educational Choice Charitable Trust in Indianapolis in 1991, and the national coordinating organization, the Children's Educational Opportunity Foundation (CEO America), headed by Fritz Steiger. Those nonprofit foundations

provide scholarships to low-income youngsters to attend private elementary and secondary schools, and to date they have generated impressive results. They also can build public support for school choice, as in Milwaukee.

Too often corporations invest heavily in public schools, while overlooking the far stronger track record of private and religious schools in educating low-income inner-city youngsters. Businessmen Theodore J. Forstmann and Bruce Kovner, who are funding thousands of scholarships for low-income youngsters in New York, Washington, D.C., and Los Angeles, "challenge entrepreneurs to become social entrepreneurs—to apply the same concept of leveraging returns on their investments to education reform."[69] Investments in private scholarship programs will reap a strong return, greatly expanding the pool of qualified workers and candidates for higher learning while reducing welfare rolls. Statutes like the one passed in Arizona in 1997 providing tax credits for contributions for private scholarships could boost support for such important programs. Until the constitutional cloud is removed from school choice and systemic education reform efforts take hold, no substitute exists for private philanthropy in the education area.

4

ECONOMIC LIBERTY

Bear along with me for a brief moment, while I attempt to define the word "bureaucracy" from the Latin word burro meaning stubborn or donkey-like; hard to move, sometimes asinine; not to be confused with jackass, caterpillar or turtle; also: an unwieldy administrative system deficient in initiative and flexibility; the more you beat it, the more stubborn it becomes.

—Taalib-din Uqdah, co-owner of Cornrows & Company, Washington D.C.[1]

"Vincent Cummins looks out from his van with the hardened eyes of a criminal," writes John Tierney in the New York Times Magazine. He describes the scene:

> [Cummins] looks left and right. No police cars in sight. None of the usual unmarked cars, either. Cummins pauses for a second—he has heard on the C.B. that cops have just busted two other drivers—but he can't stop himself. "Watch my back!" he repeats into the radio as he ruthlessly pulls over to the curb.
>
> Five seconds later, evil triumphs. *A middle-aged woman with a shopping bag climbs into the van . . . and Cummins drives off with impunity!* His new victim and the other passengers laugh when asked why they're riding this illegal jitney. What fool would pay $1.50 to stand on the bus or subway when you're guaranteed a seat here for

$1? . . . "It takes me an hour to get home if I use the bus," explains Cynthia Peters, a nurse born in Trinidad. "When I'm working late, it's very scary waiting in the dark for the bus and then walking the three blocks home. With Vincent's van, I get home in less than half an hour. He takes me right to the door and waits until I get inside."[2]

That Vincent Cummins ever could be considered a criminal is a sobering sign of the confused times in which we live. To judge from the plethora of laws, regulations, and law-enforcement resources devoted to it, one could infer that the most heinous crime in America is trying to earn an honest living. But of course, the entrepreneurs do their best to persist, even if it means operating outside the law. As John Tierney puts it, "At this very moment, despite the best efforts of the police and the Transport Workers Union, somewhere in New York a serial predator like Cummins is luring another unsuspecting victim. He may even be making change for a $5 bill."[3]

For those who are harassed in their efforts to pursue a livelihood, the system offers precious little relief. Of all the rights most Americans deem fundamental, economic liberty—the right to earn an honest living—is the least-protected. If the government tries to take away a welfare check, the recipient can go to court and tie the government up in knots. But if the government regulates a business out of existence, the courts typically provide no legal recourse. Under the current state of the law, the court need only hypothesize a conceivable "rational basis" for government regulation of enterprise—no matter how arbitrary, unnecessary, corrupt, or protectionistic.[4] The legal landscape is so bleak that I have sometimes joked darkly that instead of fighting uphill battles on behalf of embattled bootstraps entrepreneurs in court, maybe my colleagues and I should seek economic asylum for them in Russia, because at least Russia values free enterprise.

How did this bizarre state of affairs come to pass? Today's entrepreneurs who face impossible regulatory obstacles can trace the loss of their rights back more than a century to one of the most shameful Supreme Court decisions ever issued: *The Slaughter-House Cases*[5] in 1873. Following the Civil War, the newly emancipated slaves opened businesses and competed in the labor market. In an effort to maintain a servile labor supply, southern state legislatures passed the "Black Codes," which restricted such essential economic liberties as freedom of contract and private property ownership. The Reconstruction-era Congress responded by protecting such rights in the Civil Rights Act of 1866. Because the law was of doubtful constitutionality, Congress incorporated those protections among the "privileges or immunities" of citizens in the 14th Amendment. But that vital protection didn't last long. When Louisiana enacted a slaughterhouse monopoly that drove competing butchers out of business, the butchers took their cases to the Supreme Court, which by a 5–4 vote ruled that the 14th Amendment's "privileges or immunities" placed no substantive restraints on state power.[6] As a result, except for a brief period during the early 1900s when courts invalidated excessive economic regulations under the due process clause, federal courts have accorded nearly unlimited deference to government regulators, even if they eviscerate economic opportunities.[7]

One of the core goals of the Institute for Justice is to litigate cases and chip away at the foundations of *Slaughter-House* until economic liberty is restored as a fundamental civil right. But an essential precondition must exist before we can expect to establish the appropriate rule of law: Americans must revitalize the work ethic and the value we once placed on enterprise. Today's debate is filled with feel-good euphemisms like "respectable work" and "living wages"—as if some types of work are below a person's dignity. And in today's regulatory climate, people must obtain licenses and pay fees for the "privilege" of operating a business—as if work and business are some entitlement bestowed by a government agency.

It seems we have forgotten the old Biblical parable: give a person a fish and he'll eat for a day; teach a person to fish and he'll eat for a lifetime. To truly enable people to emancipate themselves from poverty, we must rediscover the old and simple truth that work—any kind of work—is inherently ennobling, and that it is the only sure means to economic self-sufficiency (an insight that at last is beginning to inform welfare policy, discussed in the next chapter). To translate that understanding into reality, we must once again establish the opportunity to work or pursue a business as a fundamental right and not a mere privilege; and to make that right meaningful, we must remove obstacles that separate people with little skill or capital from economic opportunities.

And we need to do so now more than ever. Even with a strong economy, large areas of serious unemployment persist. University of Chicago sociologist William Julius Wilson observes that "[f]or the first time in the 20th century, a significant majority of adults in many inner-city neighborhoods are not working in a typical week."[8] The unemployment rate for blacks consistently is double or more than that for whites; indeed, despite three decades of race-based affirmative action, the black-to-white unemployment ratio has grown from an average of 2.06 to 1 during the 1960s to 2.76 to 1 in the 1990s.[9] Moreover, blacks are over-represented in occupations where demand is shrinking, particularly industrial jobs.[10]

Unemployment has huge spillover effects. As Wilson remarks, "A neighborhood in which people are poor but employed is different from a neighborhood in which people are poor and jobless."[11] Wilson chronicled the multiple dimensions of the urban joblessness crisis in his 1996 book, *When Work Disappears*. He warns:

> Neighborhoods plagued by high levels of joblessness are more likely to experience low levels of social organization: the two go hand in hand. High rates of joblessness trigger other neighborhood problems that undermine social organization, ranging from crime, gang violence, and drug trafficking to family breakups and problems in the organization of family life.[12]

Long-term joblessness can perpetuate itself intergenerationally. "In the case of young people," Wilson observes, "they may grow up in an environment that lacks the idea of work as a central experience of adult life—they have little or no labor-force attachment."[13] Moreover, "[i]nner-city black youths with limited prospects for stable or attractive employment are easily lured into drug trafficking and therefore increasingly find themselves involved in violent behavior that accompanies it."[14] The link between joblessness and crime appears acute: the ratio of blacks to whites involved in serious violent crimes is 3 to 2 during adolescence, and rises to 4 to 1 by the late twenties; but among employed men, by age twenty-one there is no difference in violent crime rates between blacks and whites.[15]

The challenge of redressing joblessness is made more pressing, yet more difficult, by welfare reform, which emphasizes transitioning people from dependency to work. The dimensions of the challenge are staggering: as Fred Siegel points out, after World War II, New York City had one million manufacturing jobs and a quarter-million people on welfare—but today, it has 850,000 people on public assistance and only 300,000 manufacturing jobs.[16] "The success of the new welfare law," my colleague Chip Mellor has pointed out, "depends on creating jobs for the people who will eventually lose their public assistance. Recommendations typically call for job training and public-works employment. Yet there has been little effort to create jobs in the private sector—especially the kinds of jobs suited to aspiring entrepreneurs."[17]

A growing and diverse movement is mobilizing to confront that economic imperative. At a recent annual convention of the National Urban League, Hugh Price, the organization's president, pronounced economic empowerment "the next civil rights frontier." After the Civil War, Price observed, blacks started businesses, such as barber shops, grocery stores, and hotels. Inner-city blacks need to return to that focus, he declared, because the "endgame in a capitalist society like ours is economic power." The traditional civil rights movement "was about knocking down barriers and pushing people into employment and politics. What we haven't done with the same focus, but what we must do in the final analysis, is get positioned in the American economy as full-time players."[18]

Black Muslims have always championed economic self-sufficiency, and more recently black Christian churches across the nation are making community enterprise a central part of their ministries.[19] Leaders of eight major black denominations representing sixty-five thousand churches resolved at a December 1996 meeting of the Congress of National Black Churches to use their pulpits to expand job training and placement, foster small businesses and entrepreneurs, and pressure public schools to prepare students for work and business.[20]

"In almost every black community the church is the oldest, strongest, and most viable institution," declares Rev. James R. Samuel, pastor of the Little Rock AME Zion Church. "One of the most pressing needs in the black community is economic empowerment. It becomes a natural leap of logic to connect the two." Rev. Calvin O. Butts III of New York's Abyssinian Baptist Church is blunt: "Forty acres and a mule was right. You've got to own the acreage, own the means of capital. We must help our people become billionaires."[21]

Entrepreneurial success stories abound, often despite overwhelming odds. By creating a community yellow pages and calling business owners to the pulpit every Sunday, Rev. Samuel's ministry has helped launch and sustain businesses in Little Rock. Tired of making $320 a week working at a truck wash, Keith Hilliard used Samuel's pulpit to announce an auto detailing shop, which now grosses between $100 and $400 a day and employs two teenagers. Another congregant, Diane Commander, left her receptionist job to open a flower business.

Other churches are helping create seed capital. Rev. Jonathan L. Weaver, pastor of the Greater Mount Nebo AME Church in Upper Marlboro, Maryland, launched a Collective Banking Group consisting of more than one hundred black churches in the Washington and Baltimore areas. Congregants are asked to bank at certain institutions, which in turn agree to make special considerations on business loans and mortgages and pour capital into economically disadvantaged areas. "There has been a paradigm shift," says Weaver. "Our churches have transcended politics to focus on improving the economy in our communities."[22]

A different way of thinking is taking place as well on many Indian reservations. Often written off as hopelessly impoverished and dependent on federal government aid, tribes that have declared economic independence are developing into bastions of free enterprise. Twenty years ago, Chief Phillip Martin of the Mississippi Band of Choctaw Indians started luring manufacturing businesses to the reservation. The first was an automobile harness plant for Ford Motor Company. "I believe in doing things yourself, being responsible for that," Martin declares. "We couldn't have afforded to fail. If we had failed that first contract we'd have been finished."[23]

They succeeded, and more plants followed. Focusing on work rather than welfare, incomes on the reservation have quadrupled since 1970. The tribe plowed profits into a casino and eighteen-hole golf course—and soon, a theme park, once the seventy-four-year-old Martin finds the right roller-coaster. The reservation's unemployment rate is 3 percent, and the tribe is forced to import workers from western Alabama. "We're running out of Indians!" Martin exults.[24]

"Factories are not the answer," retorts Nancy Jemison, the Bureau of Indian Affairs planner in charge of economic development. "They are culturally inappropriate." Not so, say tribes like the Oneida Nation near Green Bay, Wisconsin, which has thrived by building a casino and diversifying into manufacturing and service industries. Unemployment is 4.2 percent, and the tribe has parlayed profits into roads, housing, health care, and education. Or the White Mountain Apaches, who bring in a million dollars a year through hunting, whitewater rafting, and rock-climbing. The BIA bureaucrats "don't understand what economic development is," says the tribe chairman, Ronnie Lupe. "We take the lead here."

Another important step in rekindling the entrepreneurial spirit in economically blighted areas is providing business training to young people. One organization, the National Foundation for Teaching Entrepreneurship (NFTE), founded in 1987 by a former high school teacher, Steve Mariotti, provides entrepreneurship training to kids from economically disadvantaged backgrounds in New York, Washington, Wichita, Chicago, and other cities. NFTE works through inner-city schools to develop business curriculums and, even more important, to teach and assist high school students to open their own businesses. The kids learn how to develop business concepts, write business plans, buy wholesale, and market their products. Seeing the pride and confidence in the young entrepreneurs' faces at the annual NFTE award ceremony engenders hope for the future.

But the potential for bootstraps entrepreneurs—upon whose shoulders the economic future of our nation's cities largely rests—is circumscribed by a network of often crushing regulatory barriers. The regulations are kept in place by a powerful and reactionary coalition of labor unions, liberal politicians, government bureaucrats, and sheltered businesses determined to keep newcomers out, whatever the cost.

The story of Vincent Cummins' commuter van business illustrates the enormous opportunities that bootstraps capitalism make possible— but also what misguided and sometimes ill-motivated government policies render impossible.[25] Every day in Brooklyn and Queens, fleets of commuter vans, most of them owned and operated by enterprising immigrants like Cummins, provide safe, reliable, low-cost transportation to between twenty and forty thousand people. The vans not only take people to work, but put people to work, providing excellent entrepreneurial and employment opportunities for people who have few skills and little capital. But because the vans threaten the heavily subsidized public bus monopoly, the Transportation Workers Union—operating through its patrons on the City Council—have turned the van owners into outlaws. Every day the entrepreneurs face the prospect of heavy fines, seizure of their vans, even jail—a Kafkaesque spectacle taking place right in the shadow of the Statue of Liberty.[26]

But the van drivers' ordeal exposes only the very tip of the regulatory iceberg. Laws and regulations at every level of government stifle competition and entry into myriad jobs and occupations, driving people into unemployment or the underground economy and draining inner cities of vibrant enterprises. Such rules are cutting off the bottom rungs of the economic ladder, with devastating consequences for people with the fewest resources, particularly minorities and the poor.[27]

Most of the rules are imposed by state and local governments acting through unelected regulatory agencies.[28] In many instances, the rules serve no legitimate public policy objectives but instead protect existing businesses or public monopolies from competition. My colleagues and I recently published studies of barriers to entrepreneurship in seven cities.[29] Our findings: regulatory barriers to entrepreneurship—from red tape to heavy fees to occupational licensing to monopolies to zoning—are ubiquitous. Even more disturbing, the cities that most seem to need new businesses—older cities with declining industrial bases and increasing unemployment—tend to maintain the most onerous and anticompetitive rules.

In Boston, for example, my colleague Dana Berliner found that "start-up businesses often face a convoluted, onerous and expensive regulatory process"—and that the city has responded, all too typically, by creating "eight different offices that offer assistance at speeding the bureaucratic process, rather than actually eliminating unnecessary requirements."[30] Likewise, she found that despite suffering high unemployment, high poverty, and empty buildings, "Detroit is plagued by an intimidating bureaucracy, stifling and expensive rules and a lack of easily obtained information."[31] Berliner recounts the story of one downtown business that wanted to expand, but was turned down because it couldn't provide off-street parking—despite the fact that the surrounding streets are nearly deserted.³² My colleague Chip Mellor's study of New York City—the capital of the capitalist world—found a "bewildering array of laws and regulations that prevent or stifle honest enterprise"—which may account in no small way that while the city's "formal" economy lost forty thousand jobs in the late 1980s and early '90s, the underground economy flourishes.³³ My study of San Diego found nonprofit groups like ACCION International eager to provide "microloans" to fledgling enterprises that lack credit histories—yet hamstrung by state regulations that treat them the same as large commercial lenders.³⁴ The catalog of barriers goes on and on, discouraging storefront enterprises as well as such classically American avenues of entrepreneurship as street vendors, child-care services, and taxicab businesses. Little wonder that once-flourishing inner-city business districts have been turned into economic wastelands.

The reflexive response to the dearth of minority business enterprises has been to create massive set-aside programs. Though doubtless those programs have moved some minority-owned companies into the mainstream, like most forms of race-based affirmative action programs they tend to concentrate their benefits on those who possess substantial resources. Moreover, like most welfare programs, they tend to perpetuate dependence rather than to foster independence.³⁵ Still, the arguments of those who oppose set-asides ring hollow so long as regulatory barriers to entrepreneurship remain widespread. As Walter Williams remarked in his pathbreaking book *The State Against Blacks*, "[T]hose clamoring against quotas assume that the economic game is being played fairly. It is not being played fairly. It is rigged . . . in a way particularly devastating to blacks."³⁶

So long as regulatory barriers to honest enterprise remain in place, our nation cannot fulfill its promise of opportunity. Going about the task of making good on that promise requires eliminating some particularly vexing barriers, as the examples below illustrate.

ENTRY RESTRAINTS

Leroy Jones perspired under the hot Colorado sun, a harness supporting a tray of cold beverages tugging at his neck. He removed his hat and stood silent along with thousands of other people at Coors Stadium, and a tear welled in his eye as the National Anthem was played. It reminded him of the American Dream—his dream. But there was no time to think about that then; the baseball game began, and he had sodas to sell.

Hawking Cokes at Coors Stadium isn't what Leroy Jones wanted to be doing. Along with three partners—African immigrants Ani Ebong, Girma Molalegne, and Roland Nwankwo—Jones decided several years ago to start a business, Quick-Pick Cabs, to serve poor areas of Denver that the three existing cab companies ignore. Like most promising capitalist ventures, the prospective company offered both a desired service and a chance to make a profit. The partners are experienced cab drivers with access to capital and customers.

With all that in hand, Quick-Pick approached the Colorado Public Utilities Commission for the required "certificate of public convenience and necessity." The three taxicab companies sent their lobbyists to oppose the application. Jones and his partners were overwhelmed by red tape. The verdict from the PUC was the same as for every applicant for a new taxicab permit in Denver since World War II: application denied. So instead of launching their own enterprise, Jones and his colleagues were consigned to work not for themselves but for others. "Every time I worked for someone else," Jones laments, "I felt limited in scope and in imagination."[37]

Jones' experience is not atypical. Government-conferred taxicab oligopolies exist in most cities across the country, effectively curtailing entry into a business that typically requires relatively little capital or formal education. In Washington, D.C., where restrictions on entry are few, most cabs are owned by their drivers. In New York City, by contrast, the cost of one of the limited numbers of taxicab "medallions" has risen as high as $200,000, with the result that few newcomers can open a taxicab business.

The restrictions on taxicab permits typically are defended as necessary to protect public health and safety. In fact, that objective is served more effectively by driving examinations, vehicle safety inspections, and insurance requirements. Arbitrarily limiting the number of taxicab permits, by contrast, merely protects existing businesses from competition.

In most cities, prospective taxicab companies must demonstrate to the satisfaction of a government agency that their services are required by "public convenience and necessity." That standard is subjective and nearly impossible to satisfy, and the process is rigged in favor of existing taxicab companies, who employ armies of lawyers and lobbyists to protect their turf.

The same is true of other businesses into which government limits entry, particularly commuter vans, trash hauling, and street vending. The costs to consumers, taxpayers, and entrepreneurs is enormous. A 1974 study by the U.S. Department of Transportation, updated to reflect current dollars, estimated that the restrictions on entry and price competition in the taxicab industry cost consumers nearly $800 million annually and that removal of the restrictions would create thirty-eight thousand new jobs.[38]

Another avenue of entry-level entrepreneurship is home-based businesses, which are proliferating in light of technological advances and the desire of parents to stay home with their children. Such enterprises particularly have provided entrepreneurial outlets for women: 70 percent of home-based businesses are owned by women, who start 300,000 home businesses each year.[39] Partly as a result, the number of businesses with a female owner will have jumped from 26 percent in 1980 to half of all businesses in the year 2000. It's "a revolution," remarks home salon owner Joanne Cornwell, "not from the top down, but from the bottom up."[40]

But local zoning regulations often limit—or prohibit outright—various types of home-based businesses. Home-based child-care centers often face onerous restrictions—despite the fact that affordable and accessible child care is essential in order for people to work. Overzealous health and safety regulations often prevent the sale of home-made food products—as Linda Fisher, the "Muffin Lady" recently discovered.[41] Each morning before dawn, Fisher would load up a red Radio Flyer wagon with six dozen warm muffins and deliver them to businesses in Westminster, Maryland. She cleared four hundred dollars a month— enough to keep Fisher and her fourteen-year-old son off welfare.

But the county health department sent out three sanitarians (not to be confused with "samaritans") with a cease and desist order, threatening possible prosecution and fines of one thousand dollars per day, for failure to obtain the proper license and inspection. "I thought that was cute," quipped Fisher, "because the state's attorney's office was a customer of mine." After a fuss in the media, the local fire department allowed Fisher to bake her muffins in its kitchen, and she's back in business. But thousands of home-based entrepreneurs are technically outlaws for operating home offices, sewing pillows, or baking apple pies.[42]

Sometimes lawsuits challenging entry restrictions are successful. In 1989, I represented shoeshine artist Ego Brown in a successful challenge to the District of Columbia's Jim Crow-era ban on street-corner shoeshine stands.[43] A few years later, a federal court ruled in favor of another of my clients, entrepreneur Alfredo Santos, striking down the Houston Anti-Jitney Law, which was passed in 1924 at the behest of the streetcar industry. "The purpose of the statute was protectionism in its most glaring form, and this goal is not legitimate," declared Judge John Rainey. "The ordinance has long outlived its ill-begotten existence."[44]

But the current state of the law usually provides little solace for prospective business owners, no matter how unnecessary or protectionistic the economic restraint. Such was Leroy Jones' fate in Denver: despite the fact that the taxicab monopoly served no public purpose, the trial court refused to strike it down.

But while the battle was bogged down in the court of law, Jones and his partners opened a second front in the court of public opinion. There they met with greater success: John Fund's searing *Wall Street Journal* editorials, an emotional CBS "Eye on America" segment, and the sharp focus of local news media brought the bureaucrats to their knees even as they were prevailing in the opening round of litigation. The state capitulated and agreed to open up the Denver taxicab market. After years of seemingly hopeless struggle against powerful opposition, Leroy Jones' dream finally came true.[45]

But something else happened to Leroy Jones and his partners along the way. They came to realize that their fight was about something even more important than their own cab company: it was about the freedom of every individual to earn a share of the American Dream.

So in the midst of their struggle, even as their enterprise remained a far-away dream, they did something symbolic: they changed the name of their company from Quick-Pick Cabs to Freedom Cabs. Today Freedom Cabs is a thriving enterprise in Denver, operating a fleet of cars and vans and employing dozens of drivers. Meanwhile, following Denver's example, Indianapolis and Cincinnati deregulated their taxicab markets.

But similar barriers block new enterprises in every state and city across America, and few entry-level entrepreneurs have the resources the fight the bureaucratic leviathan. Until the presumptions of law operate in favor of those who wish to create enterprises instead of those who would deny them, we cannot truly claim to have freedom of enterprise. "Economic liberty is the framework by which we are free," Leroy Jones proclaims, "and I believe that every American should join hands and fight for it."[46]

OCCUPATIONAL LICENSING LAWS

Dr. Joanne Cornwell chairs the Africana Studies Department at San Diego State University. But like countless black women over the past six centuries, she also styles hair. Not just as an avocation: Cornwell is a third-generation entrepreneur, providing hair styling services like her mother and grandmother before her. Cornwell has also taken her business acumen a step further, having devised and trademarked a new hairlocking technique called "Sisterlocks." The beautiful, low-maintenance hairstyle is perfectly suited to the needs of working black women. Cornwell offers Sisterlocks at her home-based salon and markets training materials nationwide so that others may apply her techniques.

Across town, Ali and Assiyah Rasheed operate a popular salon called the Braiderie. There they provide hair-braiding styles performed by artisans who, like Assiyah, are African immigrants. The Braiderie provides employment opportunities to otherwise unskilled immigrants as well as highly desirable hairstyles to satisfied customers. The Braiderie has never been the subject of a consumer complaint or health and safety violation.

The two businesses are exemplars of America's free enterprise system. Except that, like Vincent Cummins, Cornwell and the Rasheeds are all economic outlaws, their activities evoking from the government not applause but condemnation—and exposure to fines and criminal prosecution. Their crime: operating without a cosmetology license.

Without a license, Joanne Cornwell cannot open a salon outside her home or lawfully provide training to others; the Braiderie, meanwhile, has been cited by state law enforcement officials for "aiding and abetting" unlawful activity.

The braiders are not alone in their predicament. Nearly five hundred occupations, covering about 10 percent of all jobs in the country, require licenses from state boards[47]—not only highly skilled professionals who have a direct impact on public health and safety, but occupations entailing few risks. As Taalib-din Uqdah, president of the American Hair-braiding and Natural Haircare Association quips, "We're not doing brain surgery. We're braiding hair." Not just physicians but barbers, beauticians, plumbers, landscape architects, interior designers, and myriad other occupations require permission from the state in the form of occupational licenses.

The qualifications for licenses typically are determined by agencies comprised of members of the regulated profession, with the coercive apparatus of government at their disposal. Not surprisingly under those circumstances, the rules often are not narrowly tailored to protect public health and safety but instead are onerous and subjective, the better to restrict entry into the profession.

Occupational licensing affects prospective professionals in two ways. First, people who lack the skills or resources necessary to take prescribed courses and pass the examination cannot lawfully offer their services to the public—no matter how proficient they may be. For instance, African immigrants may know more about hair-braiding than any of the state's examiners—but unless they take the required hairstyling courses and demonstrate proficiency in services unrelated to their specialty, they cannot pursue their craft. Second, the rules prohibit or severely limit the ability of paraprofessionals—people who focus on subspecialties, such as paralegals or birthing midwives—from offering their services directly to the public, often at a lower cost than licensed professionals. The economic consequences of limiting job opportunities in this manner are breathtaking, particularly for people who lack the resources to navigate or challenge the system.

Cosmetology licensing is a classic example of economic protectionism inflicted under the guise of public health and safety regulation. In California, as in all fifty states, practitioners who perform any type of hair care must obtain cosmetology licenses, requiring time-consuming and expensive (between five and seven thousand dollars) training in approved cosmetology schools and passage of a written and practical examination. Neither the training nor exam require any knowledge whatsoever of hair-braiding, but do require proficiency in all manner of techniques and practices (such as chemical straightening, cosmetics, and eyebrow arching) that are not only irrelevant but sometimes utterly antithetical to hair-braiding. To what effect? Not consumer protection: in 1996, the California Department of Consumer Protection found that the Board of Barbering and Cosmetology spends an annual $4 million enforcement budget on fewer than ten cases of actual physical harm for the entire cosmetology industry each year. Meanwhile, hairbraiders must spend thousands of dollars and hundreds of hours on irrelevant training—or operate outside the law. Accordingly, the multi-million dollar hair-braiding industry exists largely underground. The practitioners then must remain small in order to escape detection, and cannot gain access to capital. When entrepreneurs are forced to function outside the mainstream economy, says Joanne Cornwell, "you don't have access to business development opportunities. You don't develop the business ethic that is going to be needed to be successful on a larger scale."[48]

Joanne Cornwell and the proprietors of the Braiderie are determined to avoid that fate. In January 1997, the Institute for Justice filed a lawsuit challenging the constitutionality of the cosmetology licensing requirements as they apply to hair-braiders.[49] The braiders scored an opening-round victory the following May when federal Judge Rudi M. Brewster refused to dismiss the lawsuit. Finding that only the sanitation and hygiene requirements—comprising only 4 percent of the required curriculum—have any relationship to hair-braiding, the court concluded that the plaintiffs could proceed with their claims that "there is no rational connection between the vast majority of the [cosmetology board's] required curriculum, and that it acts as a barrier to the entry of African hair stylists into their chosen profession."[50]

For the braiders and tens of thousands of others fighting arbitrary barriers to entrepreneurship, the struggle continues. "Economic liberty profoundly affects the lives of real people," Cornwell declares. "When you stifle economic liberty in a community, you do violence to that community."[51]

The personal stakes are huge. "It's not just about business and money," declares Cornwell. "It's about our empowerment." For Ali Rasheed, co-owner of the Braiderie, the prescription is simple. The regulations were "never made to benefit me," he observes. "I'd rather have the government leave me alone."[52]

Little chance exists that Rasheed will get that wish. But perhaps more realistic—and ultimately just as satisfying—would be a rule of law that requires a rational relationship between government regulation of economic activities and legitimate health and safety objectives. In a nation doctrinally committed to freedom of enterprise, that does not seem too much to ask—and indeed, is precisely what our Constitution requires.

WAGE REGULATIONS

When the supposedly revolutionary Republican Congress passed an increase in the federal minimum wage, liberals crowed with satisfaction over their huge triumph for poor people. But scratch the political surface and one finds that poor people were neither the primary catalysts for the law nor its prime beneficiaries. Rather, the movers and shakers behind the minimum wage increase—as with many economic regulations—are labor unions.

Wait a minute, you ask: doesn't an increase in the minimum wage—and indeed, even more hopefully, the creation of an even higher minimum "living" wage—help poor people? Sure it does: for those whose labor warrants higher wages and whose employers can afford to pay them. But for those who lack competitive skills, the result is unemployment.

Raising the minimum wage does not necessarily raise unemployment generally, explains Alan Reynolds, director of economic research for the Hudson Institute, but makes it "harder for three groups to get their first jobs: teenagers, blacks and single mothers trying to get off welfare."[53] Even though the national unemployment rate remained roughly the same in the two quarters following the increase in minimum wage from $4.25 to $4.75 per hour in September 1996 (it was raised again a year later to $5.15), the unemployment rate for teenagers increased from 16.6 to 17 percent, for blacks from 10.5 to 10.9 percent (as usual, about twice the national average), and for women heading families from 8.5 to 9.1 percent.

For people who lack job skills or experience, the main bargaining chip is wages. Minimum wage laws make work illegal below a certain wage level. They destroy for unskilled people their only competitive edge—and thereby give higher-skilled workers an artificial advantage. For that reason, minimum wage laws traditionally have been a favorite tool of those who want to keep competitors out of the labor market— whether white supremacists in South Africa and the Jim Crow-era American South, or labor unions seeking to protect their high wages against non-union competition.

Far more nefarious than minimum wage laws are "super" minimum wage laws. Many state and local governments require wages above those mandated by the federal government—invariably resulting in high rates of unemployment. Even worse are state and federal "prevailing wage" laws, such as the Davis-Bacon Act, that eviscerate any chance for un-skilled workers to compete for low-skilled construction jobs. The Davis-Bacon Act and similar laws at the state level are a major barrier to entry-level employment, particularly for minorities.

When the Clinton administration cast about for experts to help defend the Davis-Bacon Act against a constitutional challenge mounted by the Institute for Justice,[54] it called upon Norman Hill, who was happy to extol the law's virtues.[55] Hill is president of the A. Phillip Randolph Institute, which he describes as the "African American arm of the trade union movement." Hill worked previously for the AFL-CIO, and before that, the Illinois Socialist Party.

Hill acknowledged that repealing the Davis-Bacon Act, which requires "prevailing" wages on federal construction contracts would place unionized firms at a competitive disadvantage. In most urban areas the Davis-Bacon wage rate is set by union wages, which nonunion firms have to pay in order to compete for federal contracting work. As a good union ally, Hill wants it to stay that way.

But not for the law to extend to his own organization, which is nonunion. "Given our own budget limitations," Hill testified without a trace of irony, "we ourselves cannot afford to pay the same level that in most cases a union can."

So instead, like thousands of other small firms around the country, Hill hires young or inexperienced workers, pays them a little less, and gives them the skills that allow them to go on to higher paying jobs in the future. If a contractor tried to do that under Davis-Bacon, it could wind up owing huge sums in back pay or debarred for three years from competing for federal contracts. That's why five black contractors from Seattle joined forces with three public housing groups in the Institute for Justice's effort to finally lay the sixty-six-year-old law to rest.

Not only does the law require super-minimum wages often dictated by union collective bargaining agreements (with hourly rates such as forty dollars for carpenters and twenty-two dollars for general laborers), it also forces companies to adopt union job classifications and work practices—literally forcing nonunion firms to become *inefficient* in order to do Davis-Bacon work.

Not surprisingly, the law costs taxpayers lots of money. The Congressional Budget Office reported in 1994 that repeal would save $3 billion every year in unnecessary contract costs. It also makes it difficult for small, nonunion firms to compete.

Even more disturbing, the law destroys job opportunities for tens of thousands of low-skilled workers, for whom the construction industry traditionally has provided plentiful entry-level job and informal training opportunities. The widespread industry practice of hiring low-skilled workers as "helpers"—which even the government's union contractor witnesses use outside the Davis-Bacon context—is prohibited. Under Davis-Bacon, entry-level workers can be trained and paid less than skilled workers only as part of an approved apprenticeship program, and even then their numbers are limited.

That means if companies can't afford an apprenticeship program, they can hire unskilled workers only by paying skilled laborer rates. "So to that degree," the Department of Housing and Urban Development's John R. Fraser candidly testified, "you're either one or the other. Or you're not working."

For unskilled inner-city workers, it's mostly the latter, despite a federal law that requires contractors performing construction work in public housing to provide employment and training opportunities to as many residents as possible. Davis-Bacon thwarts that requirement. In the late 1980s, HUD awarded a $23 million contract to renovate 332 public housing units at Kenilworth/Parkside in Washington, D.C. Much of the work required few skills. Many residents applied for jobs, reports Diedre Williams of Kenilworth/Parkside Resident Management Corporation, one of the plaintiffs, but "not one of them was hired for a construction job as a consequence of the Davis-Bacon Act's requirements. None received training. This was a tremendous waste of opportunity for our residents, who had to watch this huge project being staffed entirely by workers outside of the housing development."

If the law was merely unfair and irrational, the plaintiffs wouldn't stand a chance in court. But the plaintiffs have something more; in fact, the proverbial "smoking gun." For not only does Davis-Bacon have a profoundly adverse *impact* on minority companies and workers, that was precisely its *intent*. That ratchets up considerably the judicial scrutiny.

The law's sordid pedigree traces back to 1927, when a contract was given to an Alabama firm to build a post office in the Long Island congressional district of Rep. Robert Bacon. As Rep. Clayton Allgood described it, "That contractor has cheap colored labor that he transports, and he puts them in cabins, and it is labor of that sort that is in competition with white labor throughout the country."

The spectacle of cheap colored labor out-competing his unionized white constituents for jobs was too much for Bacon. He had already advocated in the immigration context what one enthusiast called "a quota system" against people "who are for the most part not of the white race and who, because of their lower standards of living, are able to compete at an advantage with American workers."

Now Bacon took aim at migrant black workers, about 750,000 of whom were moving north and looking for work. Because most unions excluded them, the main competitive weapon blacks were able to wield, as the National Urban League described it in 1930, was "individual bargaining—by selling the individual workers to the employer, securing thereby positions that worker as a Negro would not be eligible."

Davis' goal was to destroy that competitive edge. His first two legislative efforts failed, but in 1931—with the Depression raging and a public works spending spree waiting to be carved up—he finally succeeded. The law had an immediate and enduring impact: although the black unemployment rate in the construction industry was the same as for whites when the law was passed, it immediately grew greater and has remained so ever since. If the court finds that Congress would not have passed the law in the absence of racial animus, the government will have to prove it is narrowly tailored to a compelling government interest—a nearly impossible burden.

In reality, the law is raw economic protectionism. Under Davis-Bacon, all contractors on federal construction projects of two thousand dollars or more must pay "prevailing wages," calculated by thirty bureaucrats at the Department of Labor who do nothing but make tens of thousands of wage determinations county-by-county across the country. Theoretically, unions dictate wages only where they have 50 percent of the local market, but in practice this share can be 25 percent or less. That means in most big cities, the amount federal contractors must pay all their workers is set not by law or competitive bidding, but by union collective bargaining agreements.

That gives unions a huge edge, and they are tenacious in protecting it. The dollar stakes are huge: Davis-Bacon applies to fully one-fourth of all construction work in the United States. The impact is multiplied by state prevailing wage laws in about three dozen states—and by seventy other federal statutes that incorporate Davis-Bacon requirements.

The unions flex their muscle even to excise minor deviations from Davis-Bacon, working their will mainly through compliant Democrats. In 1992, President George Bush suspended the law in hurricane-ravaged areas of Louisiana, Florida, and Hawaii, lowering costs of reconstruction and creating an estimated five to eleven thousand new construction industry jobs. But rescinding the suspension was one of Bill Clinton's first acts as president.

If the Democrats are union-beholden, many Republicans are merely spineless. Though faced with a painless chance to shave billions off the national debt and to create thousands of new jobs, northeastern Republican congressional defectors constantly stymie Davis-Bacon reform. As the *Washington Post* reported after one such attempt failed in 1996, "Davis-Bacon is considered sacred by the construction unions, and the effort to repeal it immediately mobilized labor on Capitol Hill." Gloated the AFL-CIO's Peggy Taylor, "The Republicans have accomplished almost nothing, and we feel we've played an important role in that."[56]

But repeal efforts move closer to success every year. The Davis-Bacon lawsuit illustrates a convergence of interests among blacks and conservatives. Take plaintiff Joe Ellis, a black self-made businessman who started a small concrete sawing company eight years ago with thirty-four dollars. Forcing him to pay twenty-four dollars an hour for even the simplest tasks, Davis-Bacon has nearly destroyed his company, and he is down to a single employee. During his deposition, Ellis erupted at the government's lawyer: "That's my company. Why should somebody else come in and tell me how to pay my people, and what I have to do? Why? That's my company."

For Beth Aaron, who works for Willie Electric Company in Oakland and serves as secretary of the Bay Area Minority Contractors Association, the issue has an even more urgent human dimension. Several years ago, the company was performing work at a San Francisco public housing development. A young black man came up to the company's president, Chris Albert, and asked for a job. Albert explained that Davis-Bacon required high prevailing wages, and he couldn't afford to take a chance on an unskilled person with no job history.

The young man came back two days later, offering to work for less money. "I won't tell the law," Aaron remembers him saying. "I mean, I'm a drug dealer, and I just want out of it. I want to make a better life for me and for my mom and for my little sisters and brothers. And I think you guys offer it to me." But Albert couldn't.

Aaron's eyes brim with tears as she finishes the story. "Two days later the young man was shot and died. Maybe we couldn't have prevented that. But maybe we could have."

I asked Beth Aaron what she makes of the fact that most liberal politicians, including Jesse Jackson, support Davis-Bacon. "If Jesse Jackson were to show up here," she replied, "I would explain reality to him."

A BRIGHTER DAY FOR ECONOMIC LIBERTY?

With economic barriers like those I have described—restrictions on new businesses, occupational licensing laws, wage regulations—it is remarkable that any new enterprises get started. The impact of regulations is exacerbated for those who lack the time, resources, or knowledge to traverse the regulatory miasma. Little wonder, as my colleague Chip Mellor reports, that in cities like New York, as much as 20 percent of the economy is underground.[57]

We cannot afford that kind of fate in America, a land built by entrepreneurs. Small businesses today reportedly employ a larger percentage of people than the Fortune 500. Technology is making start-up enterprises easier every day. Regulations should not destroy what free enterprise has built.

A couple years ago, following a joint speaking engagement before the James Madison Institute in Tampa, Florida, Leroy Jones and I appeared together on a local television show. We talked about Jones' successful struggle to topple the Denver taxicab monopoly and to start his own business, and about the larger context of regulatory barriers to entrepreneurship.

Toward the end of the show, the host turned to Jones and said, "I'd like to ask you about something else. Before the show, I heard you mention that you were feeding one hundred families. What social program are you involved with?"

Jones shook his head with equal measures of bemusement and frustration. "You don't understand," he replied. "It's not a *program*. I'm a *businessman*. Those people *work* for me."

We will know that our nation has fulfilled its great potential when Americans think once again of enterprise, rather than social workers, as the best and surest means of making sure every person goes to bed with a full stomach and a roof overhead. But that requires protecting vigorously the basic economic liberty that is every American's birthright—every American's *civil* right.

ACTION PROPOSALS

1. *Federal economic liberty legislation.* Pursuant to its authority under the 14th Amendment, Congress should pass an "Economic Civil Rights Act," along the lines of the Civil Rights

Act of 1866, to protect essential economic liberties as freedom of contract and the right to earn a living in a chosen occupation. State and local governments may regulate such activities, but only if such regulations are necessary to ensure public health or safety. The government should have the burden of proving that restraints on the pursuit of a livelihood are necessary, rather than the present burden on aspiring entrepreneurs to demonstrate that economic regulations have no rational basis.

2. *State and local economic liberty legislation*. Similarly, state and local governments should enact Economic Liberty Acts making enforceable the right to earn an honest living. Apart from such legislation, state and local governments should review all existing regulations of entry into businesses and professions—occupational licensing laws, business licenses, fees and taxes, zoning restrictions, wage restrictions—to determine whether they are necessary to protect public health and safety. Requirements of demonstrating "public convenience and necessity" to open a business such as taxicabs, commuter vans, or trash hauling should be repealed. On a broader level, local governments should make starting a small business as simple as possible, and should not discourage home-based businesses. Additionally, business and occupational regulations and the boards that administer them should be periodically sunsetted— that is, allowed to lapse unless there is express legislative reauthorization for their continued existence.

3. *Empowerment Zones*. The concept of enterprise zones— many of which have been created by federal and state governments in economically blighted areas—focused heavily on tax incentives to lure businesses. Empowerment zones, as envisioned by the American Community Renewal Act, are far more comprehensive. Their economic component emphasizes removal of regulatory barriers to start-up enterprises created by people living within the empowerment zones. A key component is inducing state and local governments to suspend

regulations restricting entry into businesses and professions. Such action is an appropriate part of the bargain when state and local governments seek federal funds.

4. *Repeal the Davis-Bacon Act.* The Davis-Bacon Act destroys tens of thousands of entry-level jobs in the construction industry and costs taxpayers billions. It should be repealed, along with "baby" Davis-Bacon Acts in three dozen states that parallel federal requirements. Some legislators, and even Vice President Al Gore, have suggested raising the "threshold" that triggers Davis-Bacon requirements (from $2,000 to, say, $200,000). Though a worthwhile step, it would not exempt most government contracts. No justification whatsoever exists for Davis-Bacon except blatant labor union protectionism. That apparently is more than enough for liberal Democrats and weak-kneed Republicans, but is not a worthwhile explanation for the people who bear the law's enormous costs.

5. *Expand federal antitrust laws to local governments.* The only monopolies that are impervious to market forces are those that carry the force of law. Yet the federal Sherman Act, which is supposed to root out anticompetitive business practices, has limited applicability to local governments—even where the government itself operates business activities and shuts out competition.[58] Congress need not expose local governments to monetary damages, but should allow competitors to challenge and remove anticompetitive local government regulations, even if they are authorized by state law.

6. *Expand tax deductions for home-based businesses.* An estimated nine million Americans run businesses from their homes. But present Internal Revenue Service Rules allow business deductions only if taxpayers use the space "exclusively" and "regularly" as the principal place of business or trade. What about a kitchen that also is used to cook family meals? Or an office that also is used by children for homework? IRS rules need to reflect contemporary realities (wouldn't that be

refreshing?), and to encourage rather than discourage legitimate enterprises in the home. Senator Christopher Bond (R-MO), chairman of the Small Business Committee, has introduced legislation toward that end.[59]

7. *Encourage community development corporations.* About two thousand nonprofit community development corporations now exist nationwide to leverage public and private funding to foster startup enterprises and provide low-cost homeownership opportunities in economically blighted areas.[60] Often those organizations are civic outgrowths of corporations who believe a larger economic base is beneficial. More businesses and philanthropies should invest in such efforts as a means of providing the infrastructure for community revitalization. Public officials should make sure that laws and regulations (such as tax laws and zoning requirements) do not inadvertently constrict their activities.

8. *Remove barriers to microlending.* State and federal lending regulations should recognize a new species of business loans: microloans (loans to start-up businesses ranging from a few hundred to a few thousand dollars). Usually provided through nonprofit organizations, community development corporations, and banking consortiums, microlending is often subjected to the same onerous rules and reporting requirements that apply to ordinary commercial lenders. Microlenders should be freed to the fullest possible extent from government regulations to allow them to provide desperately needed capital and to creatively meet the special needs of people who have little credit history.

9. *Overturn the Slaughter-House Cases.* For a century and a quarter, the *Slaughter-House Cases* have been a blight on American jurisprudence. Since its founding in 1991, the Institute for Justice has viewed each of its economic liberty cases as a small step toward chipping away at *Slaughter-House* and restoring a rule of law hospitable to economic liberty.

In winter 1995, we convened in Monterey, California for a remarkable conference of two dozen leading constitutional scholars, along with Nobel economics laureate Milton Friedman, to plot the demise of *Slaughter-House*. The effort has attracted support from all parts of the philosophical spectrum, including American Civil Liberties Union president Nadine Strossen and former Clinton administration solicitor general Walter Dellinger. Pondering the revival of legal protections for economic liberty, Justice Antonin Scalia once admonished, "[T]he task of creating what I might call a constitutional ethos of economic liberty is no easy one. But it is the first task."[61] Through cases featuring such heroes of economic liberty as Joanne Cornwell, Leroy Jones, and Vincent Cummins, we are trying to do just that.

5

COMMUNITY RENEWAL

They never should have put able-bodied people in this mess. At least the criminal lives for crime, but these people have lost all their motivation.

—Mr. Diop, an African immigrant who manages a hotel in New York City[1]

"Oooh, I was mad," recalls Opal Caples. "They said we had to start working for our welfare check! I said, 'How could they do this to us?' I didn't feel it was right, to take our money—that's for our children."[2]

Today Opal Caples is no longer a welfare mother—she is a working mother. The transformation in public policy that effectuated that change is nothing short of breathtaking. It seems almost impossible that fewer than fifteen years have passed since Charles Murray published his classic *Losing Ground*, documenting what everyone but the policy elite already knew—that welfare produces both economic and spiritual poverty—and urging that the most sensible and compassionate thing to do was not to try to mend it, but to end it.[3] Over the past few years— under a Democratic administration—the central pillar of the welfare state has collapsed. Welfare is no longer an entitlement. As a result, tens of thousands of people who worked sporadically or not at all are fending for themselves. That in turn has kindled what the *New York Times'* Jason DeParle calls the birth of "a new civic energy."[4]

The progress has been swift and dramatic, leading some to draw sweeping conclusions about the demise of welfare. "What we have seen is that welfare is not like a mountain, but like a balloon," says the Heritage Foundation's Robert Rector. "Prick it and it will almost collapse."[5] And so it appears; yet we should harbor no illusions about the difficulties ahead, for many crucial questions remain unanswered. Can people who have few skills and little workforce experience cut it over the long run? What will happen to marginal workers if the economy sours? Will success come as easily for the millions of people who remain on the welfare rolls? What will happen to people who cannot make the transition from dependency to work? And amidst it all, will politicians have the stomach to apply the tough medicine necessary to keep welfare reform on course?

The answers to many of those questions depend in large measure not so much upon the nuances of welfare policy but upon the structural societal underpinnings necessary to make reform work. For even more debilitating than the impact of welfare on individual lives is its broader corrosive effect upon community institutions that nurture individual development and sustain people in difficult times. A half-century of welfare state policies have destroyed functioning communities in inner cities across America. We must rebuild those communities for the welfare reform revolution truly to have widespread and enduring effect. While the two preceding chapters discussed essential pillars of successful communities—schools and enterprises—here we turn our attention to the less tangible yet vitally important concept of community itself.

Opal Caples' teetering journey from dependency to autonomy illustrates the breadth of the challenge. "I've always been *able* to work," she observes. "I just don't always *want* to work." Now she has no choice: in order to support her three daughters, Caples cleans a lab at Sinai Samaritan Hospital in Milwaukee. Her attitude toward her work is fairly positive. "I like this job," she says. "Every job I had, you always had someone gawking over you. This job ain't like that." It pays more than welfare did, provides benefits, offers upward mobility, and provides a sense of independence: "You're doing for yourself."

But then it fell apart. Caples had a fight with her boyfriend, who moved out. Her cousin, who had been minding her daughters while Caples worked, found a job, so Caples lost her daycare arrangements. She didn't report for work or call in for three days, which normally would cost her job. But Caples found alternative child care and asked the hospital for leniency, and her supervisor agreed to plead her case. Still, even if Opal Caples makes it this time, there is no guarantee the fragile foundation of her new life won't crumble again.

The community resources that people like Opal Caples once might have looked to often are not available. Most people in her circumstances have little developed human capital, because skills and work habits are not passed down or transmitted through educational institutions. Many women have no husbands. Family support is scarce and fleeting. Daycare and transportation are difficult and unreliable. Community charities are strapped. But as a result of welfare reform, observes Jason DeParle in his analysis of Opal Caples' situation, "The one route no longer open to her is to simply return to the rolls. She's striking off, on shaky legs, into an uncharted, postwelfare world."[6]

It is not just for people newly emancipated from welfare that community structures need to be rebuilt; it is for coming generations of children born into a bleak existence, where the odds of success or even survival are often long. The *Washington Post* recently profiled two young black men from the District of Columbia, Antonio "Tony" Pipkin and Tyrone "Tye" Curtis. Their story is remarkable not because they suffered adverse fates, but because they survived the inner-city streets and are going on to college.[7]

To do so required enormous luck and savvy. Tony and Tye grew up in a northwest Washington neighborhood where gangs, drugs, and guns claimed many of their peers. Since 1990, more than 130 people— mainly young black men—were killed within a half-mile of their homes. "Hanging around the block," Tye recalls, "is like waiting to die."

More than anything else, what helped Tony and Tye survive and find a way out was a community program called Martha's Table, a nonprofit after-school program that drew the boys in and offered a safe haven from the dangerous streets around them. The program provided them with food, tutoring, games, and positive role models, inspiring in them motivation and self-discipline.

As *Post* reporter Gabriel Escobar explains, "intervention by counselors at Martha's Table was a safety net that would be stretched over and
over again during the critical high school years, when both teenagers
went through crises."[8] The program helped them move from a dangerous high school to a better one, and helped as they encountered
problems in school or with the law. The investment paid off: in August
1997, the boys packed up for Southern University in Baton Rouge,
Louisiana, where they will embark on a new and potentially far brighter
chapter in their lives.

The type of support Tony Pipkin and Tye Curtis received once
again should be the norm, not the exception. It should come from
families, neighbors, churches, and community organizations. To get
there requires removing two types of barriers: those that impede self-
sufficiency by fostering dependency, and those that obstruct the
formation of vibrant communities. We are well on our way to eliminating the first set of barriers, but have a long way to go in reviving vital
institutions in the inner cities.

WELFARE REFORM

Only a few years ago, it seemed that welfare was so huge and entrenched
that we could never hope to get rid of it. By 1993, reports Robert
Rector, total federal and state spending on welfare programs totaled
$324.3 billion—requiring an average $3,357 in taxes from every tax-
paying household in America.[9] By contrast, in 1929, total welfare
spending was $90 million, or $813 million in 1993 dollars—a cost of
$6.68 per person in 1993 dollars. As late as 1964, welfare spending
totaled only $34.9 billion (in 1993 dollars)—an amount that would
increase tenfold in less than thirty years.[10] In the single decade of the
1960s, the proportion of Americans on welfare grew from 1.7 to 4.1
percent.[11] The massive welfare programs created during the 1930s
Great Depression and the 1960s War on Poverty displaced charity as
the primary means of helping poor people. Moreover, as Rector points
out, the structure of welfare programs created huge disincentives to
work and marriage.[12] Charity, work, and marriage are casualties of the
welfare state that will endure long after the system is restructured.

Still, the essential requisite is taming the welfare beast itself, a process that has been underway for several years but whose pace lately has picked up sharply. Even before national welfare reform legislation was enacted, the Clinton administration had given forty-three states permission to conduct welfare experiments.[13] Then in its 1996 welfare reform, Congress decreed that states devise reform plans by July 1996, moving half their caseloads into jobs within five years. It set five-year lifetime welfare limits for most beneficiaries, and turned most federal welfare spending into block grants.

Within those parameters, states possess—and are exercising—tremendous discretion and flexibility. Twenty-five states, for instance, have created "diversion" programs—one-time cash payments to help families through financial emergencies and keep them off welfare. Virginia's program provides about $1,100 for transportation, housing, utilities, child care, or medical expenses, and prohibits beneficiaries from applying for benefits for at least 160 days. So far, 83 percent of the families who received diversion benefits have stayed off welfare.[14]

The results of the stern federal edicts are head-spinning. As Hanna Rosin observes in *The New Republic*, "Unforgiving deadlines have done more to push people off the rolls than decades of nurturing and cajoling."[15] Within one year of welfare reform—before time limits in most states kicked in—the welfare rolls plummeted by 1.45 million to 10.7 million recipients, a nearly 12 percent decline. Wyoming's welfare population was reduced by 49 percent; Tennessee's by 29 percent. By May 1997, the percentage of Americans on welfare fell to 4 percent for the first time in twenty-seven years, down sharply from the peak of 5.5 percent only a few years earlier. Before 1993, there were only two years in the sixty-year history of the federal welfare program that as many as 250,000 people dropped from the rolls; by contrast, 1997 was the third consecutive year in which at least one million people left welfare.[16]

Why so much progress so fast? For Charles Murray, "My interpretation is that the rhetoric worked": get-tough edicts began to have an effect even before they were implemented.[17] The American Enterprise Institute's Douglas J. Besharov views the demise of welfare as a legal entitlement as a seminal step in stemming the tide toward greater dependency. That in turn led to an increase in what Besharov calls the "hassle factor": instead of treating welfare as automatic, welfare officials in many states began putting would-be recipients through their paces, requiring serious work-search efforts and the like.[18]

Whatever the explanation, it seems that the toughest welfare reform programs have reaped the greatest returns. Two programs in particular merit special attention: Wisconsin and New York. Among welfare reform efforts, Wisconsin's is perhaps most far-reaching: on September 1, 1997, cash assistance essentially ended. "The system that will take its place," as Jason DeParle describes it, "goes to unprecedented lengths to construct a safety net not around a check but around a job."[19] The program allows virtually no exemptions to the work rule, but it provides child and health care to all low-income working families. The program is expensive—so far, more expensive than welfare—and some might quarrel that the supplemental public benefits simply substitute one form of dependency for another. But the program gambles that a fundamental difference exists between welfare dependency on one hand and working with public support on the other.

So far the gamble seems to be paying off, tracing back to reforms implemented by Gov. Tommy Thompson several years earlier.[20] The first step was "Learnfare," which conditioned welfare checks on children attending school. The state implemented aggressive diversion policies, counseling applicants on alternatives to welfare and requiring sixty hours of job searching before eligibility. The state then placed beneficiaries into community-service job-readiness activities, with "pay-for-performance" that docked beneficiaries if they failed to show up.[21] The policies have reaped impressive results.[22] Even as the nation's welfare caseload was rising in the early 1990s, Wisconsin's was falling sharply. In the ten years between 1987 and 1996, the number of families nationwide receiving Aid to Families with Dependent Children (AFDC) increased by 14.3 percent; during the same period in Wisconsin it fell by 49.2 percent, more than twice as much as the next-most-successful state (Michigan, whose dependency declined 22 percent). Rather than slowing after the most-employable people left the welfare rolls, the trend continued throughout 1997, with Milwaukee's AFDC caseload shrinking by 2 percent each month and the rest of the state by 5 percent per month.

New York's program places greater emphasis on public-sector jobs, but the transition from dependency to productive livelihoods is proceeding far more briskly than even the most optimistic sage could have predicted. In addition to intensely screening welfare eligibility, the Guiliani administration has created a Work Experience Program that has placed over thirty-five thousand people in jobs sweeping the streets, tending parks, and cleaning graffiti. Between March 1995 and November 1996, the city reduced its welfare rolls by 18 percent, from 1.16 million to 951,000. The city estimates that the program has netted savings of $175 million—and gained extra labor that would have cost $600 million if performed by unionized workers. Less tangibly but perhaps most important, it has reinvigorated the work ethic and contributed to civic pride.[23]

The transition from dependency to work is not easy. As Heather MacDonald reports in *City Journal*, the average cumulative stay on welfare is *thirteen years*,[24] long enough to destroy spirit and initiative. Among welfare recipients, half are high school dropouts, nearly one-third call their health only fair-to-good, more than half report a history of domestic abuse, between 5 and 20 percent acknowledge substance-abuse problems, and half of long-term recipients have *never* held a legitimate job.[25] Yet as William Julius Wilson has pointed out, the paradox that presents itself is that while inner-city joblessness and dependency have created serious attitudinal and behavioral barriers to work, many poor inner-city residents still believe strongly in individual initiative as the surest means to upward mobility.[26] In other words, the ambition to work somehow remains alive; the challenge is how to transform that desire into reality.

Given the depth of the problems—problems created largely by misguided public policies—it is neither realistic nor fair to rely solely on a sink-or-swim policy to transition people from dependency to work. The support programs that have proven most successful in this regard are those that focus on changing people's attitudes and behavior, making them ready for the work world and unleashing their motivation.

Private companies that employ entry-level workers—spurred by enlightened self-interest in a tight labor market—are recruiting and training workers from the welfare rolls. Companies like Aramark, Marriott, and Pep Boys have experienced mixed success in transforming welfare recipients into able workers. But those trainees who successfully make the transition often become some of the most enthusiastic employees.[27]

Often, intermediaries are necessary to prepare welfare recipients for the work culture. One successful program is the janitorial training program operated in Washington, D.C. by Goodwill Industries. The two-week program trains welfare recipients how to clean buildings; but equally important, it motivates them to work. As the *Washington Post*'s Katherine Boo explains, "What statistics can't convey is the psychic struggle at the base" of the effort to transition people from welfare to work. In the basement classroom near East Capitol Dwellings, the city's largest public housing complex, she reports, "the ethos of the working world collides hard with the ethos of street and defeat," leading literally to a battle "for the souls" of welfare recipients.[28]

The battle is waged by Tony Cutro, a fifty-three-year-old entrepreneur who rose from sweeping streets in New York City to operating a small string of cleaning companies. "Everyone here may need a break," he says to his students. "But employers aren't looking to help you; they wonder whether you can help them. You can. Work together. Do more than you're paid to do. And I promise, your life will change."

Cutro drums into his students the importance of punctuality and grooming. He inspires pride in a job well-done. He teaches them how to fill out job applications. Goodwill then helps the graduates find jobs, sometimes at or just above the minimum wage. Despite personal problems and harsh demands, by the end, all but five of the thirty-nine students in a recent class stayed with the program—and earned a chance to begin climbing the ladder to self-sufficiency.

A related but different approach is Strive, a job-readiness program based in east Harlem with nineteen sites around the country. At a modest cost of $1,500 each, Strive takes in the hard-core unemployed— 25 percent of its clients are ex-offenders, and most have other serious problems. But over twelve years, Strive has put nearly fourteen thousand people to work; and more important, after two years 80 percent of its graduates are still working.[29]

Several features make Strive different from other programs. Its instructors themselves have traveled the road from the streets to work.

It focuses not on job skills but behavior and attitude. And it follows its clients for a lifetime.

The tradeoff is the program's high attrition rate: in a typical three-week class, thirty to thirty-five people will sign up, twenty-five will show up, and between twelve and fifteen will graduate. The goal is to rid welfare recipients of the pervasive and debilitating "victim mentality," and to transform them from the kind of people who employers turn away without a glance to the kind of people they hire. A major reason for the attrition is the program's no-nonsense attitude, which mirrors the work world: show up late, disobey the rules, and you're out. But for those who stay, the promise is great.[30]

What about the people who don't make it? Though the successful transition to work for even many of the hard-core unemployed has surprised skeptics, we can afford to harbor no illusions that everyone will make it, given that even a successful program like Strive has a dropout rate approaching two-thirds. In a sobering *New Republic* article entitled "Under the Underclass,"[31] Dana Milbank profiled Marriott's widely-hailed "Pathways to Independence" program, which recruited, trained, and hired welfare recipients. Initially, the results were extremely impressive: after one year, 77 percent of the program's graduates were still employed in steady jobs. But when Marriott recruited deeper into the welfare rolls, the results were disappointing: in the class Milbank followed, despite fairly strict screening criteria and Herculean efforts by the classroom instructor, only twelve of sixteen participants graduated, and only seven were still working less than a year later (a similar class reported even more dismal results). Given that three dozen children were depending on their parents' success in the program, those results are depressing—and probably not promising enough to keep a private company like Marriott invested in the effort.

Milbank raises the painful question: "What will happen to the most disadvantaged among the poor?"[32] With welfare no longer providing a safe harbor for those unwilling to support themselves, the remaining alternatives are even more socially destructive. "If you're going to reach this population, you need a lot more involvement," says Christa Richardson, the spirited Marriott trainer who ran the class profiled by Milbank.[33] But such involvement goes well beyond what corporate

America can accomplish, and indeed beyond the easy reach of public policy. That makes it all the more imperative that we rebuild social institutions that can effectively tend to more systemic problems.

Still, it is just as important not to retreat from certain basic lessons: that perpetual welfare is toxic, and that requiring people to work for their sustenance is not punishment but liberation. We do not know yet exactly what accounts for the drop in welfare rolls; we do not know how much further progress is possible. But it would be tragically misguided if in the name of compassion we turned back. If anything, the progress in improving people's lives should embolden our determination to end the welfare state altogether.

For as Charles Murray observes, "The interventions of outsiders—whether they be government social workers or church volunteers or socially conscious employers—requires a receptive client." A receptive client requires first, "that she is not already deeply habituated to the life she lives"; and second, that "the client knows she is in dire trouble unless she gets her life in order."[34] The two are related: we can prevent the habituation of dependency only by making dependency a difficult and unattractive status. To do so requires tough government policies.

Yet the opposite seems to be taking hold as the Clinton administration reverts to old-Democrat ways and Republicans grow weak in their resolve to fight for systemic welfare reform. Already the administration has issued regulations forbidding states from requiring community service work in exchange for welfare payments, requiring them instead to pay minimum wages (or, in the case of most public-sector jobs, much higher Davis-Bacon wage rates). And the 1997 budget bill redefined "work" requirements to include going to school or receiving training.[35] Together, those and other loopholes from the original bill make a lie of "ending welfare as we know it," and threaten ultimately to defeat the progress underway.

"The current welfare war is a bitter one with millions of hostages—poor children," declares Marvin Olasky, one of the nation's leading experts on philanthropy.[36] "Liberal supporters of the status quo do not want to hear how welfare sometimes maintains bodies, but frequently kills the spirit," Olasky charges. But reformers often succumb in the face of liberal charges that they lack compassion. "Conservatives need to realize that cost is not the main reason to fight governmental welfare policies," Olasky urges. "The real trouble is that they are too stingy in what is truly important: treating people as human beings."

Olasky's prescription is apt: "The real need is for leaders who are hardheaded, but also tenderhearted." Compassion is a hand that helps up, not one that pushes down. It is to those intermediary, helping-hand institutions that we now turn our attention.

FAMILIES

Of all the institutions most desperately needed to rebuild our communities, the family is the central pillar. And here two essential ingredients are missing: husbands and fathers.

Those ingredients also are missing from most welfare reform prescriptions. As Wade Horn, president of the National Fatherhood Initiative, observes, "A welfare system that helps single mothers become employed, but ignores the need to promote fatherhood and marriage, may only serve to enable unmarried women to rear children without the presence of the father."[37]

That leaves the core problem unsolved, the dimensions of which are difficult to overstate. As of 1992, 68.1 percent of all black children and 22.6 percent of all white children were born out of wedlock (by 1995, the overall U.S. rate was 32 percent, up from 5.3 percent in 1960).[38] Those figures impart dire economic and social consequences. As Douglas J. Besharov and Timothy S. Sullivan report, in 1994, the median income for female-headed families with children was barely 30 percent of the income for married couples with children: $14,902 versus $47,244. About one-half of single-mother households have incomes below the poverty level, compared to only 8 percent of married-couple families. In 1991–92, about one-third of all female-headed families received welfare benefits for the entire two years, compared to only 4 percent of married-couple families. Welfare and out-of-wedlock births are mutually reinforcing: AFDC recipients are 30 percent less likely to marry in the year after giving birth than non-recipients.[39]

Yet welfare reform has been targeted almost entirely toward work and eligibility for the predominantly female beneficiary population than toward the men who could provide a way out of the bind in the first place. As James Q. Wilson observes, "It is fathers whose behaviors we most want to change, and nobody has yet explained how cutting off welfare to mothers will make biological fathers act like real fathers."[40]

How then to do so from the public policy standpoint? As Besharov and Sullivan note, current welfare policies impose at least a 15 percent penalty on married couples over single beneficiaries, creating a disincentive to marriage. They point to two possibilities within the welfare reform context: "(1) allow married couples to receive welfare or welfare-like benefits, or (2) make welfare less attractive to mothers. Any combination of the two will lower the costs of leaving welfare for marriage."[41] Federal and state welfare reform programs are making eligibility more difficult; it remains to be seen what impact the tougher standards will have on marriage and out-of-wedlock births, though early indications are modestly positive.[42] Meanwhile, twenty-four states have extended welfare benefits to two-parent households that meet income eligibility requirements.

Moreover, several states have cracked down on fathers who fail to pay child support.[43] That seems an essential part of the puzzle, given that low-income families are far more often afflicted by missing fathers. Whereas families with greater financial resources can hire lawyers to track down fathers and collect child support, poor mothers typically cannot. Without child support, those families must look to the state, endure dire financial conditions, or both. Greater child support enforcement is the only solution.

John J. DiIulio, Jr., proposes three more systemic reforms. First, he urges making welfare for teenage mothers contingent on their living in adult-supervised settings. Second, he would also tie aid in such circumstances to programs that counsel and monitor young women. Finally, he urges efforts, again centered on community programs, to induce fathers to take responsibility for their children.[44]

Increasingly, public policy is focusing on the crucial role of fathers; not just from the standpoint of compelling child support but in playing an active and positive role in their children's lives. One program pursuing that goal is Baltimore's Young Fathers/Responsible Fathers Program. After being involved with drugs and several encounters with the law, one young father, Anthony Edwards, was referred to the program by a local pastor. Now he is enrolled at Coppin State College, works for a city-run nutrition and education program, and most important, is deeply involved in his little boy's life. Last year he was allowed to have his son spend the summer with him. "I felt like Superman," Edwards recalls. "I felt like I was stepping up to the plate and being a man, finally. My son needs to see me a little more often—cooking, cleaning, ironing and taking care of the stuff that I need to do."[45] The tender pictures of Anthony Edwards and his little boy frolicking together are worth more than a million words; and they are a sight that needs to grow much more commonplace for the sake of future generations.

FOSTER CARE AND ADOPTION

One impediment to family formation is the nation's foster care system. More than 500,000 children will pass through the nation's foster care system this year, double the number a decade ago. About one-fifth never will return to their original homes. Some will be adopted, but only after spending an average of three to five years in foster care. Others will spend their entire childhoods in the foster care system. For those who do, many will end up on welfare or in jail.[46]

Twenty-year-old Twenika Huddleston personifies the vicious foster-care cycle. She and her little brother were abandoned in 1990 by their cocaine-addicted mother. Because there was not a single foster home in New York that could accommodate both siblings, they were separated and Twenika was placed in the last bed in a home for unruly girls. Over the next eight years, Twenika lived in six foster homes and two group homes, was incarcerated twice, ran away, and experienced two failed reunions with her mother. Instead, for those eight years the foster care system has been Twenika's mother, and now it is grandmother to her daughter, who was born out-of-wedlock four years ago. Now on a "trial discharge" from the system and living in her own apartment, Twenika will trade the foster-care system for the welfare system when she turns twenty-one. Somehow a flicker of ambition burns bright: Twenika is determined to become a nurse. "I ain't going to get *stuck*!" she exclaims.[47]

But a half-million other children *are* stuck. A major part of the problem is a foster care bureaucracy whose sustenance depends upon a large client base. Government social workers persistently harbor illusory hopes for "family reunification," constantly delaying the day when parental rights are terminated and children are legally eligible for adoption. Meanwhile, children languish in temporary homes. In the District of Columbia, chronic bureaucratic inertia means that children wait years for adoption into homes that are waiting for them.[48] In Kansas, fourteen-year-old Dale was placed in 130 foster homes from the time he was three years old. "Just when you unpack your stuff, it's time to move again," he laments.[49]

Largely through efforts spearheaded by the National Council on Adoption in Washington, D.C. and the Institute for Children in Boston, public policy has made positive forward strides. In 1997, President Clinton signed the Adoption and Safe Families Act, which was designed to speed adoptions for children in foster care by establishing the health and safety of children the "paramount concern," curtailing the prior emphasis on preserving biological families where parents have grossly abused or abandoned children, and creating financial incentives for states to increase adoptions.[50]

The most promising approach is privatization. Kansas has contracted out the foster care process to private and nonprofit entities, which compete for contracts on the basis of performance. The private agencies are required, for instance, to place 70 percent of eligible adoptees within 180 days and 90 percent within a year—and to keep its failed placement rate below 10 percent (compared to the 10 to 15 percent average). Not surprisingly, efforts at recruitment and advertising have soared, and children are finding good homes faster than ever before.

Until recently, another major barrier to adoptions was the widespread practice of race-matching. For years, the National Association of Black Social Workers (NABSW) maintained that placement of black children with nonblack families amounted to "cultural genocide," and their pervasive influence within social worker ranks stifled the number of interracial placements. The practical problem with race-matching is that the percentage of black children awaiting adoption vastly exceeds the percentage of black families among those looking to adopt, which led to lengthy delays in the adoption of black children despite the plentiful availability of non-black adoptive families. Fortunately, NABSW's apartheid ideology was thoroughly debunked through the pioneering research of sociologists Rita Simon and Howard Altstein,[51] which showed that interracially adopted black children were not only well-adjusted but also in touch with their cultural heritage. Still, social workers continued brazenly to engage in race-matching until the mid-1990s.

Critics of race-matching include such liberal academics as Harvard Law Professors Elizabeth Bartholet, Laurence Tribe, and Randall Kennedy, who joined as cocounsel in an Institute for Justice lawsuit challenging race-matching policies in Texas.[52] There the Mullens, an interracial family, had endured social workers wrenching from their home their little two-year-old foster son, Matthew, who they had raised since he was born addicted to crack cocaine and infected with syphilis. When they sought to adopt Matthew, the Department of Protective and Regulatory Services (DPRS) refused because Matthew was black and the Mullens were not. Instead, the social workers removed Matthew from the only home he had ever known, tried an unsuccessful same-race adoptive placement, and advertised Matthew and his brother Joseph on television. Only after the lawsuit was filed did DPRS relent. State legislators were so outraged that they changed the law to ban race-matching and to provide that social workers who violate the law can be sent to jail. Recent legislation at the federal level prohibits race-matching as well. Happily, Matthew and Joseph today are thriving as members of the Mullen family, and thousands of other children once again are being adopted into loving mixed-race homes as well.

Still, the practice persists, illustrated shockingly by a Maryland court's award of custody of two-year-old Cornelious Pixley to his biological mother, who was convicted only a few years earlier of murdering his infant sister. One of the reasons cited by the judge was that it is better for a black child to be raised by a parent of his own race, whereas Cornelious' foster mother, who wanted to adopt him, is white.[53]

Using children as pawns in social engineering schemes is reprehensible. Public policy should make the child's best interests the central focus of the foster care and adoption process. If current reforms don't work, litigation on behalf of children in foster care may be necessary to establish, once and for all, that the government may not stand in the way to the opportunity for children to be a part of a nurturing family.

COMMUNITY AND FAITH-BASED ORGANIZATIONS

Arthur Lee West jabs his finger at the young man standing before him on South Street in the most troubled neighborhood in Durham, North Carolina.

"When you gonna come see me now?" West asks the youth.

"Sunday. I'll be there Sunday," the young man promises.

West may be an adult, but he has credibility with young men on the tough streets of Durham. After all, during his own youth he joined a Chicago gang and ran with the Black Panthers. But with help from a religiously affiliated rehabilitation program, he straightened himself out, joined the Marine Corps, and raised a son who graduated third in his class at Duke University. Today he works with Operation HOPE, a program supported by various churches in Durham. West coaches a basketball team that has kept at-risk youth out of trouble. He also patrols the streets, gathering youths to play basketball and keep them out of the line of fire.

When Carl Washington, the city's Parks and Recreation Department director, heard West make a pitch at his church, he decided not only to make a gymnasium available free of charge, but also that the city should cosponsor the group. It's "one of the best things to happen in Durham for a long time," remarks West.

Reporting on the basketball program for the *Durham Herald-Sun*, Paul Bonner observes that the recreation director "is the first to admit that no government agency has been able to match West's success in gaining the attention and interest of the hardest-to-reach teens, the roughly 5 percent of all teens who are responsible for the majority of juvenile crime. But then," adds Bonner, "the agencies don't walk the streets."[54]

Exactly. What we need to improve the lives of the most disadvantaged members of society is real intervention and support, from people who have a stake in their success. Many conservatives deride Hillary Clinton for her observation that it takes a village to raise a child.[55] But there is truth in what the First Lady says.

Properly construed, the "village" doesn't mean the government, whose bureaucrats despite often-good intentions usually drive home to the suburbs before nightfall, but individuals and groups in the communities themselves. Not surprisingly, community and religious groups have spectacularly better track records than government agencies in helping people turn their lives around.[56] The goal of public policy should be to empower community organizations to do even more.

First and foremost, that means religious organizations. During centuries of deprivation, churches helped sustain black communities in America. Through the transmission of moral and spiritual values, observe Glenn and Linda Loury, a "spirit of self-help, rooted in a deep-seated sense of self-respect, was widely embraced among blacks of all ideological persuasions well into this century," ultimately culminating in the civil rights revolution.[57] Today, "churches are clearly the ideal—indeed, in most cases, the only—mediating institutions in black inner-city neighborhoods," urges John DiIulio, Jr.[58] A recent study of one hundred urban congregations by Ram A. Cnaan, professor of social work at the University of Pennsylvania, found that 91 percent actively provide community services such as day care, food banks, clothing drives, tutoring, after-school "safe haven" programs, health care, job counseling, and substance-abuse counseling. Eighty percent of the beneficiaries are not members of the sponsoring congregations; the churches provide the services as part of their religious mission.[59] Studies suggest that churchgoing substantially increases the chances that young black males will escape poverty, crime, drug abuse, and failure in school.[60] The reason is simple: changing attitudes and behavior is key to an enduring empowerment; and while that is difficult for government policies to achieve, it is part and parcel of a religious ministry.

The Lourys explain why something more than economic incentives is necessary:

> For some, the intensification of pathological behaviors among the urban poor is due to the lack of economic opportunities; for others, it is the result of disincentives created by various welfare programs. Though sharply different in their policy implications, these two positions have something important in

common. Each assumes that economic factors ultimately drive the behavioral problems, even behaviors involving sexuality, marriage, childbearing, and parenting, which reflect people's basic understanding of what gives meaning to their lives.[61]

To focus solely on economic incentives effectuated through public policy is to overlook a huge part of the challenge: the moral dimension. The Lourys go on to make the point that "encouraging 'good behavior' means making discriminations among people based on assessments that are difficult, both legally and politically, for public agencies to make." By contrast, "Voluntary civic associations, as exemplified by religious institutions, are not constrained in the same way or to the same degree."[62]

More than ever before, churches are heeding the call to civic renewal.[63] The Rev. Michael Patrick Williams, pastor of the 1,200-member Joy Tabernacle Pentecostal Church, shocked his congregants when he announced he was relocating the church from its suburban Houston home to a site in the inner city. Close to Easter 1998, a new church opened along with a multipurpose building with space for recreational activities and classrooms for ministerial training. Eventually the church also will open a day school. Rev. Williams sees all this as an essential part of his ministry. "The number-one problem in the inner city is that people have lost hope," he says. Inner-city residents "believe they are destined to have nothing in their lives but defeat, difficulty, degradation and problems over and over again without any possibility of victory or rescue."[64] He plans to change that situation for as many people as he can in Houston's blighted Third Ward.

Other churches are joining together to provide social services in a way calculated to move people out of poverty. In Dallas, the Interfaith Housing Coalition brings together 250 volunteers from twenty-eight congregations to mentor homeless people and welfare mothers to help them become self-sufficient. The program provides drug rehabilitation, housing, clothes, medical supplies, job preparation, and training in basic life skills. The coalition employs a tough-love approach that focuses on building responsibility, says founder Ben Belzer. "For most of the residents, that involves a lot of adjusting: no alcohol, no drugs, no visits from the opposite sex. No fighting or guns. They have to come to class and job search every day. They can't be late, and there are no excuses."[65] Residents typically find jobs within twenty-one working days. More important, they build self-esteem and self-discipline. Volunteer Carter Holston explains the program's success: "Nobody is paying us to come here. We're here for the right reasons—because we care about you. We get a lot out of seeing you succeed."

Few would question that it is absolutely essential to enlist civic and religious organizations in the quest to rehabilitate people and communities. To empower such organizations requires changes in public policy in one or both of two possible directions. First, government can in many instances directly involve community and religious organizations in the delivery of social services. Such efforts raise concerns among some libertarians, who justifiably fear government regulation of private organizations; and by some liberals, for whom it raises religious establishment concerns.[66] But to exclude religious organizations is itself discriminatory, and eschews a vitally important part of the solution of inner-city problems. A second alternative is for government simply to leave civic organizations alone, removing regulatory obstacles and making it easier for people to make charitable contributions. Given the gravity of the problems, both approaches merit pursuit.

Examples abound of a newfound cooperative relationship between churches and governmental entities. In Prince William's County, Virginia, the school district was trying to find ways to stem the rise in student expulsions, drugs, and gangs, and to overcome a decline in parental involvement. Superintendent Edward L. Kelly asked schools to establish partnerships with local churches, in much the same way as they have created relationships with businesses. So far, about two-thirds of the district's sixty-six schools have found church partners. The result is a surge in school volunteers, who provide after-school tutors and other types of support. "There are not many stay-at-home parents anymore," remarks Stonewall Jackson High School volunteer coordinator Debra Spaldo, adding that she doesn't care whether volunteers "are church-affiliated or not. If they can come in and help with the students, that would be wonderful."[67] Superintendent Kelly thinks the program will ease strain on teachers, compensate for lack of parental involvement, and increase community confidence in public schools. The risk of occasional religious proselytization, he concludes, is worth the support churches can provide in accomplishing the schools' educational mission.

A provision of the 1996 welfare reform legislation that was sponsored by Sen. John Ashcroft (R-MO) made it permissible for states to enlist churches to provide social services, so long as participation is voluntary. Some cities have blurred the lines between religious and public delivery of social services. The Azusa Community in Boston, for instance, provides after-school care, intensive "fatherhood" classes, and prayer meetings. The fatherhood classes include several first-time criminal offenders who are required to perform community service as a condition of parole, and the classes are jointly run by state probation officers and Azusa youth workers. No overt proselytizing takes place, but sometimes Azusa counselors or parole officers will testify about the impact of faith in their lives. Boston mayor Thomas Menino explains, "For the past four years we've been working very closely with the churches. They have a mission. They get it done."[68]

Some governments go so far as to turn over welfare checks to churches to spend on behalf of beneficiaries. At least ten states contract with religiously affiliated organizations, such as Good Samaritan Industries and the Salvation Army, to provide welfare recipients with mentors who act as a constant presence in their lives. Mississippi has invested $200,000 in a Faith and Families program that has paired 425 churches with 780 welfare clients. "The state can only provide bread for the body," says the program's director, the Rev. Ronald Moore. "We can provide the bread for the soul."[69] Texas Governor George W. Bush wants to go beyond his state's Family Pathfinders mentoring program and allow churches, along with public and private agencies, to compete directly for recipients' welfare checks. The goals of such efforts are to provide work and family support and to encourage constructive behavior and personal development.

For those who opt in, the results can be positive. Maria Gonzalez's twenty-seven years have been difficult: a painful divorce, two out-of-wedlock births, a breakdown, and homelessness. As she transitioned from welfare to work, the state provided her with day care and transportation—and also a mentor, Jan Tuls, from the Calvary Christian Reformed Church. Says Gonzalez of Tuls—who has three children and three grandchildren—"She's more of a mom to me than my own."[70]

As churches assume increasing roles in the delivery of social services, the question arises whether government aid and strings will
threaten the religious mission or the effectiveness of the programs. To
the extent that government merely includes religious entities among the
range of options that beneficiaries may choose, religious organizations
may permissibly intertwine religious teachings; but where government
contracts directly with religious groups, it usually insists that religious
activities be divorced from the delivery of services. "The question now,"
reports Joe Klein, "is whether the politicians—and the courts—are
ready to move toward a more explicit relationship: one that acknowledges that the 'faith' in faith-based programs is often the very quality
that makes them successful."[71]

Meanwhile, other faith-based programs flourish and want nothing
from government but to be left alone. Exemplary among them are Teen
Challenge and the Rev. Freddie Garcia's Victory Fellowship, two nationwide private drug rehabilitation programs. "The organizations most
effective in helping addicts to freedom are those that emphasize faith
in God and a turn from the path of addiction," says Sen. Dan Coats
(R-IN). "While many clinical approaches would emphasize 'treatment'
and would consider drug and alcohol addictions 'diseases,' faith-based
centers put the responsibility squarely on the individual, presenting
drug use as a moral choice that will lead to further physiological and
financial problems."[72]

The record backs up Sen. Coats' claims. Freddie Garcia, a former
thief and drug addict, found salvation in Jesus Christ and launched his
Victory Fellowship to save others. Since 1966, the San Antonio-based
program has reclaimed thirteen thousand hard-core addicts with its
tough-love program, working with an annual budget of only $60,000. Its
boasts a 70 percent success rate for addicts who stay with the program for
nine months, compared to a 10 percent cure rate for more mainstream
drug rehabilitation programs. Garcia wants nothing to do with government money. "I don't want no grants," he insists. "I'm a church. All I
want is for you to leave me alone."[73] Government funds mean government regulations, such as minimum space and bed requirements. "If
we are full, and somebody comes in in the middle of the night and
is willing to sleep on a couch," Garcia says, "he sleeps on the couch."[74]

Freddie Garcia's regulatory nightmare became Teen Challenge's nightmarish reality, even though it takes no public funds. Started in 1958, the faith-based drug rehabilitation program has grown to 130 chapters across the country. Its remarkable long-term cure rates—between 67 to 85 percent—prompted the National Institute on Drug Abuse to comment that "involvement with Teen Challenge is associated with dramatic changes in behavior for a substantial number of heroin users."[75]

That record didn't impress the Texas Commission on Alcohol and Drug Abuse (TCADA), which acted to shut down the San Antonio program in 1995, threatening the program's officials with jail and $4,000-per-day fines. TCADA found Teen Challenge in noncompliance with a blizzard of regulatory requirements—some utterly trivial, such as frayed carpeting on the stairs—but the essence of the charge was that the program did not employ licensed professionals or follow the state's prescribed regimen. "We use a Christ-based approach here, and it works," responded the center's director, the Rev. James Heurich. "Their programs do not. Why don't they look at our success rate?"

Meanwhile, some TCADA officials themselves were prosecuted for diverting one million dollars in treatment funds to bonuses and gifts for the agency's administrators.[76] Despite the agency's unclean hands, it took a rally of 325 people—many of them former addicts—and a threatened lawsuit by the Institute for Justice to force the agency to abandon its efforts to shut down Teen Challenge.[77]

The inevitable regulatory entanglement between the state and civic and religious programs is an omnipresent threat, but one that must be met head-on. As Sen. Coats observes, we "would be well-served if more faith-based centers were established. For that to happen, government should offer its arm of encouragement but withhold its grubby fingers of bureaucratic regulation."[78]

A nice deal if we can get it. But whether in partnership with government or independently, we need to help such programs grow in number and scope. Nor do they have to be religious in orientation, though that can be helpful in addressing the moral dimension. The central factor is that they possess a direct stake in reinvigorating their communities. That means giving people in the communities greater control over their own affairs. Why not allow community groups to deliver social services or bid for city contracts? Why not administer workfare through community organizations? If the government wants to collect trash, operate daycare centers, or provide transportation services, why not contract out to community groups?

One activist who has taken an entrepreneurial and comprehensive approach to community renewal is Kent Amos. A former Xerox executive, he gave up a profitable career to launch the Urban Family Institute in Washington, D.C., which takes a "whole village" approach to community renewal.

Amos started his crusade more than a decade ago almost by accident. His son brought home a kid from the basketball team after school. Amos found that the boy's parents had deserted him and that he had flunked eighth grade. Amos invited him to dinner, and then to study quietly with his own children in the evening. Soon others followed, until more than one hundred children eventually became Kent Amos' "children"—turning to him for mentoring, tutoring, and emotional support.[79] Now he is setting off to make the Shaw neighborhood a nurturing community for children—not only by reinventing its institutions but also by getting existing ones to work together. Shaw has eight thousand children who are supposedly served by three high schools, four junior high schools, nineteen churches, Howard University, and myriad social service agencies—but those entities don't coordinate their activities. Amos wants them to work together to provide a wholesome, positive environment in which children spend all their waking hours.

Already, Amos has pulled together mothers from a public housing development to cook dinner for all the children each evening in the community center. The kids study together and interact with positive adult role models. Amos also plans to open charter schools that offer extended hours, beginning the long process of rebuilding the community one institution at a time.

His main focus is children, who are most at risk in neighborhoods where violence, drugs, and dependency are the norm. "We try to make our children believe that we are in control, but it's not true," observes Amos. "The children themselves have the ultimate decision on almost everything they do, starting at a very young age. All I am doing is trying to get them to internalize a set of values."[80] With those values, the children can meet the challenges of a lifetime.

HOUSING

Aside from work and entrepreneurship, perhaps no greater economic incentive exists to positively transform communities than homeownership. Private property gives people an ownership stake in the community. But housing policies have operated in exactly the opposite direction, creating a new entitlement and warehousing poor people into massive government-owned or subsidized housing complexes. The now-derisive term "housing project" is all too apt, for it is a crude form of social experimentation.

One of the nation's most innovative housing experts is Howard Husock of Harvard University's John F. Kennedy School of Government. He urges a complete transformation of our nation's housing policies— and fast. Since 1962, Husock observes, the Department of Housing and Urban Development (HUD) has spent $384 billion to house the poor. The developments that house one-third of the four million families who receive federal housing assistance are often in terrible disrepair, and they concentrate and exacerbate social maladies among the urban poor. The Republican response has been to adjust the rules to actually expand the entitlement to working-class families. HUD plans to demolish 100,000 of the worst public housing units and spend nearly a billion dollars to fix existing housing projects and build four thousand new units.[81]

Reform proposals abound on both sides of the political spectrum— scattered-site public housing, housing vouchers, new housing designs. But none of those alters the nature of the entitlement or gives people an ownership stake in their housing, which is essential to community renewal. "Keeping a neighborhood safe and property values high is a common enterprise that helps hold communities together," says Husock. He explains,

> Residents fashion the civil society of their neighborhoods
> through myriad activities—organizing crime patrols, volunteering
> at a local school, or simply doing favors for neighbors—that make

an area a better place to live. Every day, citizens join in this confidence-building enterprise to reassure each other that their neighborhood will remain attractive to new buyers, will remain a good place to live and increase in value, and may provide the wherewithal to move up to a more expensive neighborhood.[82]

Husock proposes transforming HUD from an agency that provides housing for people into one that explores and facilitates the removal of impediments to homeownership. He notes that numerous private and nonprofit entities—such as Nehemiah Plan Homes in New York City and Habitat for Humanity in Atlanta—are constructing low-cost housing accessible to people with modest incomes. Some cities have relaxed rules for rental units so that poor people can afford apartments and rooms in privately owned buildings. Ultimately, Husock urges moving toward getting government out of the housing business altogether—"not primarily to save money, but to allow for the emergence of a traditional alternative: strong, even if poor, neighborhoods based in private ownership."[83]

Blocking the way, observes Husock, is "the political clout of 3,400 housing authorities scattered in congressional districts through the country."[84] Moreover, local governments stymie the supply of affordable property through restrictive zoning laws, overly burdensome building codes, development exactions, historic preservation ordinances, rent control laws, and other regulations that protect the "haves" from the "have-nots."[85]

A useful transition step is tenant management and ownership of public housing, a mechanism made possible through federal legislation sponsored by then-Rep. Jack Kemp and others in the 1980s. As the Heritage Foundation's Dr. Stuart Butler observes, tenant management emerged "not as an enlightened experiment by progressive local housing authorities, but more often than not out of a desire of desperate governments to wash their hands of a 'hopeless' project."[86] In the 1970s, Cochran Gardens in St. Louis was so infested with drugs and prostitution that observers called it "Little 'Nam." Under the dynamic leadership of a former member of the Black Panthers, Bertha Gilkey, the tenant association petitioned the housing authority to let it assume management responsibilities. Working with the police, the new managers drove drug dealers out of the development. They also hired tenants to perform maintenance work and created new enterprises—such as a catering, roofing, and daycare—to provide services in the development and the surrounding area. All told, the tenants have created more than 350 jobs.

Other public housing developments have followed a similar course. In Washington, D.C.'s Kenilworth-Parkside, where many units have been sold to tenants and others are managed by the resident management corporation, the crime rate has plummeted by 75 percent and teenage pregnancy by 50 percent. Job creation has increased rent collection, reduced welfare dependency, and brought home absent fathers.

Why the positive changes? As Butler explains, "The difference between tenant management and traditional private contracting is that the management firm consists of people who live in the project." Kenilworth-Parkside's Kimi Gray quips, "My engineer lives in the project, and when the heat goes off he gets cold, too."

Another factor, Butler observes, is that "tenants are willing to accept stringent rules from a resident corporation that they would never accept from City Hall." As Flagg Taylor and Robert B. Hawkins, Jr. observe in their recent book, *Owning the Dream: Triumph and Hope in the Projects*, strong community organizations can be built in public housing only if authorities recognize the residents' right to self-government, rather than insisting that they remain clients of the established social-service system.[87]

But in many instances that has been wishful thinking. Although several public housing authorities have actively fostered tenant management, many others have resisted it with messianic fervor. After four years of support during the Bush administration from HUD Secretary Jack Kemp, the Clinton administration tightened tenant management eligibility rules. Meanwhile, restraints such as the Davis-Bacon Act (see chapter 4) limit flexibility for tenant self-governance.

The greater the stake that people have in private property, the greater their control over their own destinies and their stake in the American system. Efforts to empower residents of public housing through greater control of their communities—and ultimately through opportunities for homeownership—are essential to rebuilding our most blighted inner cities and helping people climb the economic ladder.

PHILANTHROPY

Before the advent of the welfare state, private charities shouldered virtually the entire burden of social welfare. "During the 19th century, before the federal government ever got involved, a war on poverty, much more successful than our own, was waged by tens of thousands of local, private charitable agencies and religious groups around the country," observes Marvin Olasky. "These 19th-century warriors did not abolish poverty, but they did help millions of families to move out of it."[88]

Today, government largely handles the responsibility of social welfare. "Government welfare programs are notorious for their ineffectiveness," charges Olasky. "Private charities are not necessarily effective, but they have the opportunity to be."[89] The National Commission on Philanthropy and Civic Renewal, chaired by former Tennessee governor and U.S. Secretary of Education Lamar Alexander, underscores the vital role of philanthropy:

> Above all, private charity is able to recognize that the chief difficulty in aiding the poor is as much moral as material. . . . Government is ill-suited to provide or even supervise that type of support. Indeed, in a free society we don't really want government interfering with morals, values, individual responsibility, and behavior, let alone with the religious basis of much of morality.
>
> This is where the private sector can play a unique and irreplaceable role. It can help people to learn to live virtuously. It is this capacity for moral leadership that confers on private philanthropy the greatest comparative advantage vis-à-vis government. Individual donors and members of private and corporate philanthropies ought never to lose sight of this.[90]

Americans still contribute billions of dollars annually to charities—indeed, more than the total of federal entitlement programs. Yet despite the existence of myriad churches and local charities that are effective in helping the poor, too often they are not the object of organized philanthropy, which sometimes seems to have become part of the political establishment. The Alexander commission found that too much foundation and corporate giving is ineffective and misdirected. Private foundations, the commission says, conduct too much study, too little direct service, and too little hard-nosed evaluation; and they often prefer grand theories and government intervention to simple solutions to tangible problems.[91] Some large established charities like United Way have fallen sway to political correctness, directing funds on the basis of nebulous racial and ethnic "diversity" considerations rather than success in achieving charitable goals.[92] Moreover, "volunteering" has increasingly become an extension of government, through such programs as AmeriCorps and mandatory community service in public schools,[93] rather than a matter of individual charitable impulse.

Several leading philanthropic organizations—among them the Lynde and Harry Bradley Foundation, John M. Olin Foundation, Sarah Scaife Foundation, Randolph Foundation, JM Foundation, Jacobs Family Foundation, William H. Donner Foundation, and foundations headed by Charles and David Koch—have steered contributions toward the task of community renewal. Still, too many foundations continue to waste money on big social projects that do little to improve people's lives. Corporate and private foundations should reevaluate their missions and scrutinize the real-world impact of their contributions if institutional philanthropy is to realize its vast full potential.

As great an impact as individual charity has on the lives of people, it could grow exponentially. Most people view their tax dollars as their primary means of aiding the poor—an understandable view given the vast amount of public funds expended for social welfare. One way to increase individual giving is to provide tax credits—an idea championed by Lamar Alexander and Senator Dan Coats (R-IN).[94] The proposals would allow taxpayers to reduce their federal or state tax liability dollar-for-dollar for contributions to community-based poverty-fighting charities. The amount of money spent on such endeavors would stay the same or actually increase, but more of it would be directed by taxpayers rather than government—almost certainly increasing its effectiveness. Under that system, the "focus of the debate would change from money to power," Marvin Olasky remarks, "and that is a debate that advocates of welfare change can win."[95]

THE AMERICAN COMMUNITY RENEWAL ACT

Throughout this chapter, I have emphasized the limits of what government policy can achieve in the area of community renewal, and the necessity of private action. Still, for better or worse, government will inevitably remain a dominant player in social welfare. To the extent that it does, empowerment advocates should champion government policies that encourage individual initiative and private solutions—such as community delivery of social services, privatization of adoption, and poverty-fighting charity tax credits—and that do no harm.

A comprehensive empowerment bill, the American Community Renewal Act, could serve as a focal point for positive federal policy reform. In the 105th Congress, the bill was cosponsored by Representatives J.C. Watts (R-OK), Floyd Flake (D-NY), and James Talent (R-MO); and Senators Spencer Abraham (R-MI) and Joseph Lieberman (D-CT). The bill goes well beyond previous enterprise zones, recognizing that economic revitalization alone is insufficient for community renewal. The act would create one hundred "renewal communities," combining pro-growth tax benefits with regulatory relief, low-income scholarships, homeownership opportunities, and community delivery of social services.

Eligible areas are those with poverty rates of 20 percent or more, unemployment rates 150 percent of the national average, and most of their households having incomes below 80 percent of the national median. The communities must agree to reduce local taxes and fees and to eliminate state and local sales taxes within the zones; and to waive local and state occupational licensing regulations and other barriers to entry, unless they are necessary for public health and safety. In return, the federal government would provide capital gains tax relief and other tax benefits; give communities the power to provide public housing homeownership opportunities to low-income families; provide funds for low-income scholarships; allow income tax credits for contributions to charities providing direct services to the poor; and lessen restrictions on the ability of community and religious entities to provide drug treatment. As the Heritage Foundation's Christine Olson describes it, the American Community Renewal Act provides "an opportunity to change the direction of social policy in a way that will directly empower

Americans in troubled communities to improve their standard of living and quality of life."[96]

Imagine that: a new model of social policy reform, based not on dependency and government intervention, but on individual and community empowerment. No legislation can solve the ills of the urban poor—but it can give people the tools and freedom to solve problems themselves.

ACTION PROPOSALS

1. *Welfare reform.* Given the success to date of stringent welfare-to-work requirements, the federal government should ratchet up demands of states in return for federal welfare subsidies, with stiff penalties for noncompliance. The flip-side of the equation is to provide states with maximum flexibility in meeting the requirements. Successes like Wisconsin and New York City come only with the flexibility to address local circumstances, which vary dramatically.

Our nation's experiment with the welfare state has been disastrous in its human consequences. Defenders of the status quo are retrenching with horror stories, but politicians should recognize that welfare dependency is ultimately far more toxic than the alternative. The goal of welfare reform should be the abolition of welfare, with a safety net provided primarily through families, communities, and private philanthropy.

2. *Community service and non-minimum-wage jobs.* A key requisite of state and local flexibility is the power to require welfare beneficiaries to work for their checks. The point that is lost on those who believe otherwise is that work *experience* is as important as the actual amount of wages. So long as work is part of the welfare transition process, the requirement of minimum wages (or more-expensive Davis-Bacon wage rates) will greatly diminish such opportunities—particularly in the private sector,

but in the public sector as well. Public sector unions know that, and it is their protectionistic self-interest rather than true compassion that drives pro-minimum-wage policies. Welfare reform advocates should make exemptions to minimum wage and Davis-Bacon requirements a top policy priority.

3. *Child-care and family tax credits.* President Clinton has proposed tax credits to help working parents pay for child care.[97] Such credits will especially help welfare beneficiaries who are transitioning to work, but of course will assist all working parents. Fortunately, the president did not propose federal child care regulations. Health and safety regulations are best set and administered at the local level, and families (especially those of limited economic means) often rely on informal child-care arrangements that should be eligible for credits.

But the president's proposal doesn't go far enough. As Michael Kelly points out, "the policy as a whole is irrationally biased toward the form of child care most parents like least—institutionalized group care—and against what most parents want most: to be able to have one parent stay home."[98] The proposal gives no tax relief to such families. Republicans have proposed extending child care tax credits to families where a parent stays home to care for their own children.[99] Another possible form of family tax relief is "income-splitting," which allows a one-income family to split the income between both parents, thereby bumping them into lower tax brackets. Child-care tax credits should not discriminate against families who care for their own children, often at substantial financial sacrifice.

4. *Enlist community organizations and faith-based organizations to help people climb out of poverty.* Community and faith-based organizations often know how to fight drug addiction, train people how to find jobs, and rebuild communities—and more important, they have a vested interest in success. Federal, state, and local governments should draw upon their expertise and commitment to the greatest extent possible. Moreover, urban

policy should be guided by the understanding that community renewal requires the rebuilding of community institutions, which the welfare state has done so much to supplant.

To the extent that faith-based programs receive government funds, constitutional concerns over religious establishment can be satisfied by (a) including faith-based programs as part of a broader array of options and making participation in them voluntary; and (b) involving the government as little as possible in the internal policies and operations of the programs.[100] One way to facilitate such involvement—while minimizing bureaucratic entanglement and maximizing competition—is through vouchers (for job training, addiction treatment, child care, etc.), which beneficiaries can redeem at a variety of public or private social service agencies, including religious entities.

5. *Allow private organizations to operate unmolested.* A large number of private and nonprofit poverty-fighting entities want neither government funds nor government regulation. The remarkable track records of groups such as Teen Challenge suggest that government is better advised to tend to its own affairs than to worry unduly about private entities. Private groups should be free to pursue what works in treating drug addictions, preparing people for jobs, and so on. The government's role should be strictly limited to ensuring voluntary participation and health and safety. Government licensing and standardization does nothing to advance but much to inhibit the groups' important missions.

6. *Families.* Welfare policies should be examined and restructured to ensure that they do not undermine the one institution most closely linked to social well-being: the family. Policies that focus exclusively on encouraging mothers to work overlook the crucial responsibility and involvement of fathers. Greater efforts should be made to reduce the financial penalties on two-parent families. For single-parent families, efforts should be increased to collect child support and to encourage fathers to play a positive role in their children's lives.

7. *Foster care and adoption.* Efforts should be redoubled to move children out of foster care into loving families, bolstered by the recognition of a due process right of children to have such opportunities. Private agencies that have a vested interest in facilitating adoptions should be used more frequently. Barriers to adoption—such as restrictions on adoptions by single parents or gay couples—should be eased. The state should not be allowed to discriminate on the basis of race in adoption placements where loving families are willing to adopt interracially; indeed, Texas' model of exposing social workers to jail if they discriminate in adoption placements should be adopted by other states.

8. *Homeownership opportunities.* Private property ownership increases a person's stake in the community and in the American Dream. The government should move out of the slumlord business. To the extent government continues to operate public housing, it should give tenants a greater role in managing housing developments, and to require local public housing authorities to facilitate resident management. The goal of government policy should be to privatize public housing, encouraging the provision of private low-cost rental housing and the purchase of public housing by tenants. State and local governments should ease taxes and regulatory barriers that impede the development of private rental housing and homeownership opportunities.

9. *Private foundations.* Private and corporate foundations should take a close look at the grants they provide in aid of the poor. They should spend less on studies and more on direct provision of support and services, and demand success in lifting people out of poverty.

10. *Poverty-fighting charitable tax credits.* Policymakers at the federal and state levels should provide dollar-for-dollar tax credits for taxpayer contributions to organizations that help people lift themselves out of poverty. One model is the Arizona Education Tax Credit, which provides state income tax credits for contributions to scholarship funds. Such credits encourage tax

payers to contribute to poverty-fighting efforts and eliminate bureaucratic costs. They also help rebuild the institutions necessary for community renewal.

11. *The American Community Renewal Act.* The American Community Renewal Act provides a bipartisan, multifaceted approach to urban policy reform. It embraces several key underpinnings of positive federal policy: (a) that economic revitalization is essential but not sufficient; (b) that community renewal rests on community and individual empowerment; and (c) that although government is typically an impediment to empowerment, for better or worse it will continue to play a role, and its role should be to facilitate empowerment rather than inhibit it. For Policy makers at the federal level, the American Community Renewal Act provides a constructive complement to welfare reform. Its architects are to be commended for transcending politics, standing up to special interests, and putting people first. Even if Congress passes the bill, President Clinton will likely veto it, presenting an opportunity for vibrant debate in the next presidential election.

6

FREEDOM FROM CRIME

There is certainty in MacLean. If you do this, this will happen. Not so in Anacostia. You can just walk down the street and get shot.

—Asa McCall, a teenager who escaped
Washington, D.C. for the suburbs[1]

Twelve-year-old Darryl Hall was a bright and precocious youngster. At that age, most boys prove themselves through sports or academics. But Darryl lived in the inner city, where—far too often—the currency of adolescence is bullets.

Four years before, after his father deserted the family, Darryl's mother had moved them away from the violence-riddled Benning Heights neighborhood in Washington, D.C., to the safe haven of Oxon Hill, Maryland, where Darryl was raised mostly by his grandmother. But Darryl's mother found her new life boring, so after a few years the family moved back to southeast Washington.

There Darryl fell in with a gang called the Simple City Crew. The gang split up into warring factions, and turf was staked out through violence. Darryl was eager to establish his place among the older members of his faction. One night, Darryl accompanied other gang members into enemy territory, firing away like a gunslinger. A young man in the rival faction broke his leg while fleeing. That injury sparked retaliation, with a member of the rival faction reportedly vowing to kill "the little boy."

The rival gang made good on its promise. On January 15, 1997, four assailants chased the 85-pound youngster and his fourteen-year-old brother a block from their home. "Darryl turned off away from me," his older brother D'Angelo recalls. "I'm thinking they was gonna chase me, not him. I got halfway up a hill, I turned around, and I saw they had him. He was fighting and kicking."

The attackers threw Darryl into a car and drove him a few blocks to a ravine not far from where the boy attended Bible school, then dragged him from the car to a stream. There he was shot in the leg. As Darryl screamed, the assailants proceeded with the latest custom of the streets: they held a gun to his head, and shot and killed him, execution-style. His frozen body was found three days later.[2]

Such is the new code on the mean streets of the inner-city, in the shadow of the nation's capitol. When murder is deemed appropriate retaliation for minor indignities, when little boys trade their childhoods for guns and drugs, we all must fear for the devaluation of human life those developments reflect.

And yet, of course, it is not so everywhere. For most Americans, the news about crime is good. In 1996, violent crime dropped 7 percent nationwide, the fifth straight annual decline and the largest since the federal government started keeping track thirty-five years ago. The murder rate dropped 11 percent, bringing the homicide rate to its lowest level since 1969.[3] Those trends continued in 1997.

The recent trends reverse significantly a fourfold increase in violent crimes during the 1960s and 1970s. They seem to show that vigorous law enforcement and tough punishment work: a study by the National Center for Policy Analysis shows that violent crime has decreased in places where the possibility and duration of punishment have increased—and that violent crime has increased where the possibility and duration of incar-ceration decreased. By example, a comparison of two states, California and Texas, reveals rising crime as Texas decreased the likelihood of incarceration and declining crime as California grew tougher with prison sentences.[4] Nationally, the overall trends seem promising.

But the drop in violent crimes has not benefited all Americans equally. "America does not have a crime problem; inner-city America does," remarks John DiIulio, Jr. "No group of Americans suffers more" from the ravage of criminals than "law-abiding inner-city citizens and their children."[5]

Most Americans cannot imagine the omnipresent climate of fear in which millions of people live: neighborhoods where the streets are so violent that children cannot play outside, people can't walk the streets at night, families fall asleep to the sounds of gunfire, stray bullets in the ongoing drug wars hit innocent people[6]—and, perhaps most ominous, where sometimes police won't respond to calls for help.

Freedom from crime is the most fundamental civil right, and the protection of people and their property is the first object of government. Historically, personal security figured prominently among the civil rights movement's top priorities. In the 1940s, President Harry Truman's Committee on Civil Rights identified four basic rights of which black Americans were systematically deprived: the right to safety and security, to citizenship and its privileges, to freedom of conscience and expression, and to equality of opportunity.[7] In the past fifty years, we have made enormous strides in securing the latter three rights—but little in securing the first and most basic: freedom from crime.

Yet establishment civil rights groups have virtually abandoned that goal in favor of defending criminals. As Harvard law professor Randall Kennedy observes in his superb analysis *Race, Crime, and the Law*, "blacks have suffered more from being left unprotected or underprotected by law enforcement authorities than from being mistreated as suspects or defendants, although it is allegations of the latter that now typically receive the most attention."[8] Likewise, although murders register "strongly in today's liberal imagination when committed by whites against blacks," observes Jim Sleeper in his eye-opening book *Liberal Racism*, "more blacks in the United States are killed by other blacks in a single day than are killed by whites in a week. Yet black victim after black victim is lowered into urban America's choking soil without a word from any liberal commentator, activist, or politician, black or white."[9]

Of all the issues on which the so-called civil rights groups have strayed from their constituents, nowhere is the dichotomy between ideology and interest more stark than crime. The groups see civil rights infringements aplenty in the crime context—but their concern is over the *criminals*, rather than their victims. Groups like the NAACP Legal Defense Fund target their resources toward helping criminals escape the consequences of their crimes. Among other things, the Legal Defense Fund relentlessly challenges capital punishment. In *McClesky v. Kemp*,[10] and in proposed federal legislation called the "Racial Justice Act," it has sought to introduce affirmative action principles into criminal law, arguing (unsuccessfully so far) that capital punishment is unconstitutional on account of racial statistics: not because a disproportionate number of black *killers* are sentenced to death—the statistics don't support that allegation—but because killers of any race who murdered white *victims* are more likely to be sentenced to death. Assuming that the explanation for those statistics is discrimination—itself a sketchy proposition[11]—the appropriate remedy, it seems to me, is not to level the penalties down but to bring them up. Criminal law, above all, is no place for affirmative action. The time has come to reorient the law's focus from the rights of criminals to the basic civil right of all people to be free from crime.

In 1992, I personally experienced the breakdown of civil order in the Los Angeles riots. On the balmy evening of April 29, a colleague and I were driving through south-central Los Angeles on our way to a meeting with prospective clients in a school choice case when the riots broke out. Our car was attacked and we barely escaped with our lives.[12] But escape we did—unlike thousands of others whose lives, homes, and businesses the police abandoned to the marauders.

For me, the Los Angeles riots brought into sharp focus the glaring defects of public policy as it relates to inner-city crime. The riots illustrated a profound breakdown in the rule of law—and in respect for life and property—that infects many inner-city areas. I witnessed firsthand the urban phenomenon described by Stephan and Abigail Thernstrom: "Violence has become more casual, and perpetrators seem less remorseful."[13]

But even worse than the rioters was the conduct of law enforcement officials. That the police would completely abandon their responsibility to protect vulnerable people—while securing the affluent downtown areas—underscored the disparity in the most basic of civil rights, freedom from crime. Too often that disparity breaks down along racial and economic lines. "It is not the disproportionate impact of punishment that makes the system racist but the disproportionate impact of our failures at prevention," declares University of Southern California law professor Susan Estrich.[14] "Deliberately withholding protection against criminality," Randall Kennedy charges, "is one of the most destructive forms of oppression that has been visited upon African-Americans."[15]

The alienation that flows from the failure to protect people from crime is exacerbated by the use of racial stereotypes in law enforcement. As Kennedy observes, "Public authorities have long used race as a signal of an increased risk of criminality."[16] People who are guilty of no wrongdoing are harassed because they are "out of place" or they fit criminal "profiles" based in part on race or ethnicity. Kennedy observes that "[w]hile affirmative action is under tremendous pressure politically and legally, racial policing is not."[17] Indulging such racial generalizations exacts a price too high, for they undermine respect for law enforcement. Such tactics, Kennedy explains, "cause people who might otherwise be of assistance to police to avoid them, to decline to cooperate with police investigations, to assume bad faith or dishonesty on the part of police officers, and to teach others that such reactions are prudent lessons of survival on the streets."[18]

As in Tom Wolfe's brilliant satire, *The Bonfire of the Vanities*, many inner-city residents view police officers and prosecutors as a mercenary occupation force. Even among many law-abiding blacks, confidence in the integrity of law enforcement and the administration of justice has so eroded that they are sometimes willing to subvert the system. Cooperating with the police or pursuing a career in law enforcement or criminal prosecution is viewed as "selling out." The view, even among middle-class blacks, that the criminal justice system is racist "prompts some black jurors to be unreasonably skeptical of police testimony," Kennedy observes, "or even to refuse to vote for convictions despite proof beyond reasonable doubt of defendants' guilt."[19] George Washington University law professor Paul Butler, a former prosecutor, has gone so far as to urge black jurors to "nullify" verdicts against blacks accused of non-violent crimes. "I do want to subvert the system," Butler brazenly declares.[20]

Of course, the proposed cure is worse than the diagnosed disease. "Butler exudes keen sympathy for nonviolent drug offenders and similar criminals," observes Randall Kennedy. "By contrast, Butler is inattentive to the aspirations, frustrations, and fears of law-abiding people compelled by circumstances to live in close proximity to the criminals for whom he is willing to urge subversion of the legal system."[21]

Yet alienation is manifest. Some of it is reflected in jury nullifications: in 1995, mainly black juries in the Bronx acquitted nearly half of all felony defendants, nearly three times the national acquittal rate; in the District of Columbia, mostly-black juries acquitted 29 percent of felony defendants, nearly twice the national average.[22] Mistrust runs deep: a 1990 survey found that among college-educated blacks, 29 percent believed that the government deliberately makes sure drugs are available in order to harm black people, and 38 percent believed it might be true.[23]

Hence the paradox that at the same time as poor, inner-city people— particularly blacks and minorities—endure an epidemic of crime unprecedented in modern civilized society, respect among those same people for the rule of law and the system that supports it has eroded precipitously. All this spells what Kennedy calls a "crisis of legitimacy"[24] for our system of law enforcement. That means that the challenge of securing freedom from crime is a dual one: restoring respect for law enforcement while taking far more aggressive action to enforce the law. Plainly, current reform efforts have not been nearly radical enough to meet that challenge.

And no challenge is more urgent. The statistics are gruesome. In the 1990s, *murder has become the leading cause of death among young black males*. The murder rate for black males age fourteen to seventeen is 77.3 per 100,000—a figure three times higher than it was twenty years ago, and eight times higher for blacks than whites in the same age range. For black males age eighteen to twenty-four, the figures are even worse: the murder rate is 184.1 per 100,000, more than seventeen times greater than for whites the same age.[25] In terms of all violent crimes, the victimization rate for teenage black males is 113 per 1,000—more than 1 in 10. Nationally, 27 percent of black children (versus 5 percent of white children) think it likely they will be shot.[26]

Crime also lures black males from constructive livelihoods, and many wind up out of their communities and in prison. Among suspects arrested for murder, 54.4 percent are black, as are 59.5 percent of those arrested for robberies, and 36.9 percent arrested for drug violations.[27] Their victims are overwhelmingly black as well: 86 percent of people killed by blacks are themselves black.[28] Criminality is approaching epidemic proportions: overall, nearly one of every three black men between the ages of twenty and twenty-nine is in jail or otherwise under supervision of the judicial system.[29]

So the question arises: how do we ensure personal security and stop the scourge of inner-city crime? As with the other issues discussed in this book, the issue of crime is interrelated with other maladies. Fatherlessness and welfare dependency seem to greatly increase prospects that youngsters will engage in crime.[30] And of course the converse is true: as men are lost to crime, they abandon their families and thrust them into poverty. The dearth of legitimate economic opportunities in the inner city increases relative rewards of criminal activity—overall, blacks in their late twenties commit four times as many crimes as whites; yet among employed men, blacks and whites commit crime at equal rates. High crime rates, in turn, increase the costs of legitimate enterprises and people who patronize them. Poor education and high dropout rates lead to greater crime. Unlike more affluent people who can move away or protect themselves within secure enclaves, "inner-city blacks must rely almost exclusively on the justice system for protection against criminals," DiIulio notes. "At every level, this system has failed them."[31]

But whatever the core causes and effects, no excuse exists for the unsafe neighborhoods in which crime reigns. For people who every day fear for their lives, no greater salvation could be delivered than to make good on the promise of personal security. Here as in other areas of empowerment, the answer lies in decentralization to the community level—both to reinvigorate support for the rule of law, and to deliver law-enforcement resources into the hands of the people who have a direct stake in community tranquillity. In the pages that follow, I shall explore what seems to work—and urge reforms far more systemic than have been considered.

COMMUNITY-BASED LAW ENFORCEMENT

The first step to reclaiming the streets is to reestablish a rule of law. That means, first and foremost, acknowledging the reality of high levels of

criminality among blacks, and rejecting arguments that putting criminals in jail is discriminatory. As DiIulio urges, "The black crime gap is
real, not rhetorical or racist, and black Americans' rising fear of crime at
a time of declining crime rates must be addressed."[32] Randall Kennedy
concurs, observing that "the black law-abiding population . . . desires
more rather than *less* prosecution and punishment for *all* types of
criminals." A 1993 Gallup poll shows that 82 percent of blacks believe
courts in their area do not treat criminals harshly enough; 75 percent
favored more police on street to combat crime; and 68 percent
supported building more prisons to make way for longer sentences.[33]

That demand translates into returning vigorous, tough law enforcement to the inner cities—one block at a time, if necessary. In New York
City, massive police force has been unleashed on some of the city's most
crime-ridden blocks. Instead of merely responding to crimes, the police
have committed to becoming an integral part of the neighborhood's
day-to-day life.

Starting with a drug sweep on 163rd Street between Broadway and
Amsterdam Avenue, police have barricaded the block and stationed
officers around the clock. The officers act as armed guards and scrub graffiti. They stop unfamiliar pedestrians and motorists and turn away people
who don't have a reason to be there. Norman Siegel, executive director of
the New York Civil Liberties Union, sees "serious constitutional questions" in the blockades and recruitment of residents as informants. But
residents are able to walk the streets safely for the first time in memory.[34]

"We are here to help you and will stay as long as it takes, but you
have to use this time to organize yourselves," Officer Miguel Adorno
tells a meeting of block residents. "Alone, you will always be victims.
But with numbers, you can save this block." Reluctantly, law-abiding
citizens began to work together and with the police. "We are all afraid,
but we'll do it, even if it's just five or six of us in this building," declared
T. Houston, a forty-five-year-old hospital worker. "We'll do it because
it's a start, and we've got to start somewhere if this hell we've lived
through is ever going to end."

The 163d Street experiment is one part of a multifaceted anticrime
campaign carried out in New York City by the Guiliani administration.
Initiated by former police chief William Bratton, the effort has stream-

lined the police department's bureaucracy and decentralized authority to the precinct level. The use of computer-generated crime statistics has improved the ability to measure progress, a system backed by unprecedented accountability: precinct commanders who fail to improve crime rates are replaced; those who succeed are rewarded with greater authority.[35] The results over the first three years are staggering: as Fred Siegel reports, "nowhere has the drop in crime been as sharp and sustained as in New York City," with auto theft down 46 percent, robbery down 41 percent, and murder 49 percent—its lowest level in nearly 30 years.[36] In stark contrast, the District of Columbia—clinging to a bloated, politicized, often corrupt police bureaucracy that seems resistant to innovation and accountability—has experienced continuing high crime levels.[37]

New York City's approach exemplifies a broader law-enforcement reform effort nationwide that has two separate but related components. First, it emphasizes "quality of life," built upon the recognition that there is "a 'seamless web' between controlling petty crime and restraining major crime."[38] Associated with James Q. Wilson and George Kelling, the notion is that when broken windows go unfixed in a neighborhood, it leads to reduced respect for property and order; and when small crimes go unchecked, it encourages more serious crimes. Broadly speaking, as Fred Siegel points out, what has driven people from cities is not so much "crime per se but, rather, the sense of menace and disorder that pervade[s] day-to-day life."[39] Panhandlers, mentally ill people roaming the streets, pushers, prostitutes, and the presence of graffiti and garbage all add to an atmosphere of disorder that breeds lawlessness. By demanding higher standards of civic behavior, law enforcement authorities can improve respect for the rule of law.

New York City's efforts along those lines have gained credibility among skeptics. "Now that the City of New York has, through its policing of minor 'quality of life' offenses, posted a sign saying 'Stop,'" remarks Jim Sleeper, "many of its residents have discovered that not only is it not racist to do so, it enhances a sense of public order and helps to reduce the murder rate in poor, nonwhite neighborhoods more than anywhere else."[40]

The second component of law-enforcement reform is "community policing." In the past several decades, "police work has concentrated on reacting to crimes already committed—on rapid response to calls for service and the investigation of crimes after they happen," explains former U.S. Attorney General Edwin Meese. "Today, the emphasis of police work is expanding from the crime lab and squad car to include foot patrol and strengthening communities."[41] Originating in cities like Newark, New Jersey; Flint, Michigan; Houston, Texas; and Charleston, South Carolina, the idea of community policing encompasses high levels of citizen-police interaction, community organization, and other efforts to prevent crimes. As Siegel describes it, the approach has police officers "talking with people to establish rapport; moving miscreants on; and most importantly, establishing the common standards of behavior essential to making people feel safe."[42]

A major facet of community policing, as William D. Eggers and John O'Leary have examined, is foot patrols, or "walking the beat"— "the practice of charging a small group of officers with responsibility for a small area, [which] has hardly been seen since the 1950s." The beat system, observe Eggers and O'Leary, "increases the connection between law-abiding citizens and the police and gives citizens opportunities to express their concerns."[43]

In Indianapolis, officer Mike Elder's beat encompasses a three-square-mile area that includes two of the city's worst public housing developments. He spends a considerable amount of time each day patrolling the housing developments, neighborhood parks, and stores, and he maintains a field office in the Clearstrom public housing development. Before the beat patrol, "there would be gunfights in the project in the middle of the street in broad daylight," says one resident. After two years of the patrol, calls to police from Clearstrom dropped from 1,500 to 550. "Before Mike came in, I wouldn't dare let my kids play outdoors because of the shootings and drug deals going down at all hours of the day and night," reports a single mother who lives in the development. "People living in the projects want a normal life, too— and we're getting there."[44]

The preeminent practitioner of community policing is Charleston police chief Reuben Greenberg. When Greenberg arrived in Charleston in 1982, violent crimes were rising, particularly in the city's public housing developments. The department, Greenberg charges, "had written off whole sections of town to the criminal element."[45]

Greenberg launched an anti-crime initiative dubbed "Take Back the Streets." He created a "flying squad"—a kind of second police department—that was intended to prevent crime rather than merely to respond to it. Much of Greenberg's emphasis was in the public housing developments. Working with housing authorities, he began throwing criminals out of the housing and screening new tenants for criminal records. "No other landlord has to rent to child molesters, robbers, rapists, and arsonists," remarks Greenberg. "Why should people in public housing have to live with them?"

Greenberg worked to increase police presence in the community and police/citizen interaction by establishing four mini-stations, two of them in public housing developments; and by extending foot patrols, which already served the downtown business districts, to poorer neighborhoods. He stationed police officers in areas of frequent drug sales and photographed buyers, causing drug markets to dissipate.

The results of Greenberg's efforts have been impressive: crime has dropped by 42 percent; the last murder in a Charleston public housing development was in 1985; and the use of police force has decreased, with only one shot fired by a police officer in eight years and few complaints of excessive force. And the city has preserved its reputation as a desirable tourist destination, helping bolster its economy.

Greenberg's innovations go well beyond community policing.[46] First, he started an anti-parole unit, whose mandate was to oppose parole for every criminal who committed serious crimes with high rates of recidivism—burglaries of homes, sexual assaults, and armed robberies. A detective appears at each parole hearing, often with the victim along. After twelve years, the success rate in denying parole is 76 percent.

Second, he revived the practice of truant officers, who round up errant youths and return them to their school principals. Daytime crime subsequently was reduced by 24 percent.

Third, he instituted a program called "Operation Midnight." Recognizing that youth curfews present constitutional problems, the police department allows parents to voluntarily register a curfew time for their children. "If the mother and father say they want the kid home by midnight," Greenberg observes, "it doesn't make any difference what the ACLU says." At midnight, the police start enforcing parental curfews. Those efforts have provided a potent antidote to the epidemic of youthful criminality and victimization: in seven years, the city has not experienced a single murder by a juvenile, while two were killed.

Finally, the city pays one hundred dollars to tipsters who turn in people who are carrying illegal weapons. A large number of young people have reaped the cash rewards, helping purge guns from the schools.

Greenberg's efforts show that a city doesn't have to turn into a police state to eradicate crime. But it does have to take crime seriously and get its priorities straight. "Let the defense attorney protect the defendant," Greenberg declares. "I am not going for that crap. We look out for the interest of the victim."[47]

Unfortunately, some of what passes for "community policing" taints the concept. As Tucker Carlson reports, with the Clinton Administration's creation in 1994 of an Office of Community Oriented Policing Services within the Justice Department, the concept of "community policing" was seized upon as "an opportunity to repair the social ills inside the hearts and minds of police officers themselves."[48] The revised philosophy was epitomized by a bulletin put out by the Justice Department's Community Policing Consortium, which stated that people involved in law enforcement "must learn to recognize the power and beauty of diversity, rather than blaming our social problems on other people."[49]

The example of Nicholas Pastore, who became police chief in New Haven, Connecticut in 1990—the same year William Bratton took over in New York City—"is a cautionary tale of how 'community policing' can be dangerous in the wrong hands," says Carlson. Police and societal racism, according to Pastore, were the main causes of crime. Pastore implemented hiring quotas to diversify the department, engaged in "proactive dialogue" with lawbreakers, joined the New Haven chapter of a para-street gang called Zulu Nation and defended its leader despite his record of violent crime, took a double-murder suspect out for pizza, and handed out his business card to drug dealers in case they were victimized by police brutality. Not surprisingly, police morale fell precipitously, and so did law enforcement. In 1986, New Haven police arrested 2,389 people for drinking in public; in 1993, only thirty-four were arrested for the same crime. In 1985, police took 648 people into custody for vandalism; between 1990 and 1993, the number was zero. Finally, in 1997, Pastore resigned after he admitted having an extramarital affair with a possibly mentally-impaired hooker, and then failing to support their child.[50]

As is the case with other systemic empowerment reforms, powerful special interests often will mobilize to protect the status quo. That's what Jersey City Mayor Bret Schundler found when he tried to move cops to the beat. When the mayor was elected in 1992, only one police officer worked foot patrol; Schundler wanted three hundred. But Schundler discovered that the city's police force preferred comfortable jobs, and that the "patronage system has made assignments to street patrol intolerable." When the mayor reassigned two cops from delivering interoffice mail to walking the beat, he was slapped with a lawsuit by the police union. Schundler charges that union contracts and state arbitration laws stymie effective law enforcement. "Our crime problem is not the result of our spending too little on policing," Schundler charges, "but rather of our getting too little policing for our money."[51]

Schundler makes an important point: simply hiring more cops is not enough. For as John DiIulio, Jr., notes, "Only a tiny fraction of all cops are ever actually on patrol." Washington, D.C. has more police officers per capita than any other big city, but few of them are on patrol, and they are disproportionately assigned to affluent neighborhoods and tourist centers.[52]

With a proper focus on protecting people against criminals, community policing demonstrably holds enormous promise. But to the extent that it fails to deliver real authority into the hands of the people most directly affected, it does not go far enough. Two additional innovations merit serious consideration.

The first is private security. While most of Washington, D.C. is easy prey for criminals, certain Georgetown neighborhoods are safe— not just because the police department assigns more officers to affluent parts of the city, but because citizens have taken matters into their own hands and hired private guards. "What's unusual about these areas is that they aren't management companies or organized homeowners' associations," says Joel Gininger of Wells Fargo Guards Services. "These are just individual residents who organize for one reason: security."[53]

Residents in various parts of northwest Washington and suburban Virginia—indeed, about 85 percent of Georgetown—have assessed themselves for private security services. Between 1992 and 1995, the number of robberies in Georgetown has dropped 36 percent, and auto thefts have decreased by 10 percent even as they escalated sharply elsewhere in the city.

Reactions to private security among public officials vary. Albert C. Eisenberg, a liberal Arlington County Board member, complains that that private security "smacks of vigilantism." But Barry Malkin, captain of Washington's second police district, acknowledges that the guards "are visible, so they are a deterrent. It's more eyes and ears to tell us about more bad guys. To criminals, the guards are the same as police. When criminals see a uniform, generally they won't do something."

Obviously, private security is a viable and increasingly popular option for businesses and affluent citizens. But what about poor people? If police can't do the job, local governments should rebate a portion of municipal budgets to local community organizations for anticrime patrols. Public housing authorities should contract with resident management associations to provide security. The basic job of policing—patrolling and deterring crimes—might better be contracted out to neighborhood groups that have a vested interest in crime prevention.

Some cities have closed off streets, creating neighborhood enclaves. Since the mid-1970s, St. Louis has closed off more than one thousand streets and turned over ownership to neighborhood associations. The street closings foster neighborhood cohesiveness and have helped reduce crime. "The street has become an extension of the front yards of the abutting homes," says city planner Oscar Newman, "an area where children play and adults can meet and socialize." Neighbors learn who belongs and who doesn't and can look out for each other, recreating a lost spirit of community.[54]

Local governments might think even more comprehensively, particularly if they are concerned (as they should be) with the legitimacy of law enforcement in the eyes of disaffected communities. Just as with large-city public school systems that have grown bloated and unresponsive, so too have law-enforcement agencies. Here too we should consider true devolution: decentralizing police departments—*and district attorney offices*—along community lines, thereby literally delivering law enforcement authority and responsibility into the hands of communities.

Instead of one huge Los Angeles Police Department and a county-wide prosecutor's office with their top-down bureaucracies, each discrete community would operate autonomous law-enforcement entities, empowered to train and hire from the community and to apply community standards.

The main functions of the central police office in a community-based law-enforcement system would be administrative and strategic support and prevention of corruption. Decentralization is not a license for cronyism. In a troubling *New Republic* exposé of the Washington, D.C. Police Department, Carl T. Rowan, Jr. reveals how, in the name of "empowerment," Mayor Marion Barry systematically destroyed one of the nation's best large-city police forces through patronage and lowered standards.[55] The point is to empower *communities*, not politicians. That entails shifting power, discretion, and accountability—and the rewards or detriments thereof—into the community's own hands.

I'm reminded of the sharp sense of unreality experienced by the character played by Eddie Murphy in the movie *Beverly Hills Cop*, who arrives in that posh suburb fresh from the mean streets of Detroit. The rules are different—and should be different. Devolution of law enforcement power to the community level will accomplish two main goals. First, it would give power to the people with the greatest stake in civil order—the people who live there. Second, it would confer legitimacy upon law-enforcement officials. No more mercenaries, no more occupying armies. Unless and until current authorities can guarantee protection from crime to all citizens, they should take such steps to allow people to protect themselves.

CHILD-CENTERED CRIME PREVENTION

Major efforts must be directed toward the people most vulnerable to crime and susceptible to criminality: children.

In the aftermath of the killing of twelve-year-old Darryl Hall in Washington, D.C. emerged the Alliance of Concerned Men, a group of eight ex-felons who organized to combat crime. Capitalizing on their credibility among local street toughs, the group negotiated a peace truce among warring gangs that produced at least a momentary end to violence in an area that had witnessed 59 recent homicides in a five-block radius. Other groups organized symbolic marches and neighborhood cleanups, but as one policeman observed, "What these kids need is someone to change their hearts." Says Robert Woodson of the National Center for Neighborhood Enterprise, "Neighborhood-based, grass-roots groups, led by committed individuals who have personally experienced the problems they address, know how to instill vision and hope in young people otherwise labeled as 'hopeless.'"[56]

Some observers predict the problems of youth and crime will worsen. John J. DiIulio, Jr., has chronicled the emergence of juvenile "super-predators," youthful offenders who think nothing of engaging in criminal acts or inflicting brutal violence. He notes that juvenile violent crime has exploded in the past decade, accounting for 26 percent of the growth in violent crime. In 1994, more than 2.7 million juveniles were arrested, one-third of them under age fifteen. Even more worrisome is that as the age of criminality decreases, the number of youngsters in the relevant age ranges is growing: by the year 2006, the teenage population will top thirty million, the most in over a quarter-century.[57] Nor is the problem confined to the cities: violent crimes by juveniles involving guns and drugs are spreading rapidly to suburbs and rural areas, where law-enforcement authorities often are ill-equipped to deal with them.[58] Unless we stop the trend now, it threatens to engulf an entire generation.

District of Columbia Superior Court Judge Reggie B. Walton laments that when one combines demographics "with bad parenting, bad neighborhoods and the easy accessibility of guns, all of that fuels the problems that we see coming."[59] So long as the streets are mean and positive male role models are scarce, significant intervention must take place to ensure that inner-city youngsters do not turn to crime (or become victims of it, or both). DiIulio urges institutional placements for juvenile offenders from dysfunctional families, and a change in family law policies that focus on family preservation rather than the child's best interests. He notes that too little research exists on the effects of out-placements of juvenile offenders, but such alternatives must be explored.[60]

DiIulio also recommends the three Ms: monitoring, mentoring, and ministering.[61] Monitoring refers to community-based supervision of youthful offenders, whether by probation officers or neighborhood adults. Mentoring involves one-to-one relationships between at-risk youths and citizen-volunteers. Ministering means outreach programs conducted by religious organizations. All contribute to lower rates of recidivism and development of positive values.

Again, the solutions are interrelated. In Compton, just before the Los Angeles riots, I met with the Rev. Matthew Harris, who headed Project Impact, a mentoring program for at-risk youths in south-central Los Angeles. Harris was a strong advocate of school vouchers—not so much for educational quality, but because he feared returning the successful graduates of his program to crime-infested and gang-ridden public schools. Education is the one facet of public policy over which we have greatest control, and good schools provide both a safe haven and the tools to climb out of poverty. As a preventative measure against crime, radical education reform makes enormous sense.

VICTIMS' RIGHTS

Over the past few centuries, criminal law has shifted away from its traditional emphasis on securing justice and restitution for individual victims toward vindicating society's generalized interests.[62] The shift has moved too far, to the point where the individual victim enjoys virtually no status whatsoever in the criminal justice system. The prosecutor owes the victim no duty, and justice and restitution for the victim are subordinate goals—to the extent they are goals at all.

Again, poor people are affected disproportionately. People of means, such as the family of the murdered Ron Goldman, can hire private lawyers and pursue civil lawsuits against criminal wrongdoers. Of course, even such lawsuits are meaningless unless the criminal has resources to provide restitution.

Genessee County in New York State has pioneered efforts to alter the ordinary equation. Its law-enforcement goals, as Joe Loconte describes them in *Policy Review*, are "not merely punitive, but restorative: to help repair the harm done to victims and their families."[63] The county offers intensive victim assistance and involvement in all aspects of the judicial process, and emphasizes community service, restitution, and even face-to-face meetings between criminals and victims. Explains

Loconte, "Advocates call these efforts restorative justice, a religiously rooted philosophy that redefines crime as an offense not primarily against the state but against human beings."

Such efforts are the focus of victims' rights organizations, which over the past decade have successfully pushed twenty-seven states to protect victims' rights in their constitutions, typically providing for restitution and victim involvement in criminal prosecutions. One crucial facet of victims' rights—statements of victims at sentencing—has been struck down by the U.S. Supreme Court as unduly inflammatory in certain instances.[64] Some civil libertarians[65] contend that victim impact statements are unfair because they raise irrelevant factors and because some victims endure greater losses than others. It seems to me that criminals take their victims as they find them—a murderer of a vagrant who has no family may be lucky, but that should not excuse from the full consequences of his actions the murderer of a mother who leaves infant children behind. One life is not "worth" more than another, but the impact of one death is not the same as another. Justice is not secured when a criminal fails to pay for part of the impact of his crime. A principal object of criminal justice should be to make the victim whole.

Fueled most recently by outrage over the exclusion of victims' families from the courtroom in the Oklahoma City bombings trial,[66] a proposal to add a victims' rights amendment to the U.S. Constitution is gathering momentum. Sponsored by Senators Jon Kyl (R-AZ) and Dianne Feinstein (D-CA) and backed by the Clinton administration, the amendment would recognize the rights of victims of violent crimes to notification of and testimony at trial and parole proceedings; adjudication of cases without unreasonable delay; notification of the offender's release or escape; consideration of the victim's safety in parole proceedings; and standing to assert those rights in court.

Some observers fear that liberals support victims' rights legislation as an alternative—rather than supplement—to tough law enforcement. "[V]ictims' rights represent more than the conservative entry in the great American rights race. They are the restoration of a valuable tradition jettisoned without sufficient thought and brought back in limited form to ensure a fuller conception of justice," explains Andrew Peyton Thomas. "Even so," he adds, "the victims' rights agenda must not detract from the essential task of crime prevention. Today's unacceptably high crime rate is the product of a pervasive disregard at all levels of government for our most important civil right—that of personal security: the right not to become a victim in the first place."[67]

DRUG LAWS

As a libertarian, I have always favored drug legalization. For many years, it was for me a simple issue: the government has no business telling people what they can do to their own bodies, so long as those people don't harm others in the process. Drug use was a "victimless crime," as I saw it, and therefore not legitimately criminalized.

Over time, particularly as I have spent more time in inner cities, I have come to recognize that drug use is not victimless. First and foremost, it damages the user in innumerable ways, through debilitating addiction, distorted reality, and sometimes death. It damages the community as well, sapping its moral fiber and productive human capital. Little wonder that drugs are a highly emotional issue, particularly within inner cities. Given their human degradation, one can even understand why conspiracy theories gain currency, for a community could not willfully bring this blight upon itself.

And so a war on drugs makes intuitive sense, and such a war has been waged with fervor and massive resources. Over the past decade, federal spending on the drug war has escalated more than 500 percent, from $3 billion to $16 billion. By 1995, nearly 1.5 million people had been arrested for drug-use crimes.[68] Indeed, as Randall Kennedy observes, "The war on drugs . . . largely explains why, in recent years, the incarceration rate among blacks has exponentially superseded the rate among whites."[69] The numbers are stark: America incarcerates 3,109 black men per 100,000; by contrast, the black incarceration rate in apartheid-era South Africa was 729 per 100,000.[70]

But for all the effort, drug laws seem to have made problems worse, not better. A recent article by journalist David Simon and retired homicide detective Edward Burns brought home the dimensions of the drug policy dilemma.[71] For three years, Simon and Burns immersed themselves in the culture of a street corner in west Baltimore that is home to a notorious drug market. There they witnessed the ground level of a drug war "that has become endless and, arguably, pointless"—and literally "an absurdist nightmare."

Maryland has twenty thousand prison spaces, and ranks tenth among the fifty states in its incarceration rate. Yet in Baltimore alone there are eighteen thousand drug arrests each year, and more than thirty-five thousand statewide. Doubling the number of prison spaces—which could bankrupt the state—still would not accommodate the estimated fifty thousand heroin and cocaine users in Baltimore alone. Because most prison spaces are reserved for violent offenders, only about eight hundred of the eighteen thousand people arrested for drug offenses are incarcerated, and many of those will serve less than one year.

So the corner operates unscathed; indeed, even more brazenly than before. And the police step up their efforts, invading neighborhoods like a foreign occupying force. Many of the younger officers don't remember when the neighborhood was worth protecting, so there is little connection to the streets or people who live there. The "worst of the West Baltimore cops," Simon and Burns report, "have become brutal mercenaries, cementing their street-corner reps with crushed fingers and broken noses, harvesting the corners for arrests that serve no greater purpose than to guarantee hour after hour of paid court time."[72]

There are so many addicts that arrests are easy—much easier than with more serious crimes. But as Simon and Burns remark, "Stupid criminals make more stupid police." If drug-related arrests are as simple as catching fish in a barrel, important police skills like investigating and solving crimes erode. Meanwhile, as police resources are increasingly devoted to drug-use crimes, serious crimes escalate. In the years from 1988 to 1993, when the cocaine epidemic inflated drug arrests, crime in Baltimore rose by 37 percent, the clearance rate for shootings declined from 60 to 47 percent, arrests for rape fell by 10 percent, and the number of solved burglaries fell by a third. Meanwhile, the rate of heroin and cocaine use was the highest in the United States. The thirty-year war has reaped myriad "victories": "tens of thousands warehoused in prisons; millions of dollars of contraband dollars confiscated"—and more than half of Baltimore's adult black population under the supervision of the criminal justice system. But of course the underlying problem of drug use is bigger than ever. "If we never seriously contemplate alternatives, if we forever see the order of battle in terms of arrests and prisons and lawyers," Simon and Burns conclude, "then perhaps we deserve three more decades of failure."[73]

Nationwide statistics echo the Baltimore findings. Despite ever-escalating expenditures for the war on drugs, drug-related deaths increased from 5,500 in 1990 to 7,000 in 1993. In 1994, the number of first-time cocaine users was less than half that in 1986—perhaps due to publicity over cocaine-related deaths—but the numbers of marijuana, heroin, and LSD users were up.[74]

A study for the Cato Institute by James Ostrowski documents the sometimes-hidden costs of the drug war.[75] The black market prices of heroin and cocaine, Ostrowski notes, appear to be about one hundred times higher than pharmaceutical prices. The artificially inflated prices cause users to turn to crime to support their habits, contributing to an estimated 40 percent of all property crimes, which amounts to four million crimes per year and $7.5 billion in stolen property. The illegal drug trade also leads to about 750 drug-related murders each year, and to the deaths of about ten law enforcement officers annually. Because no quality control is assured in the black market, prohibition makes drugs more dangerous. Moreover, as Ostrowski points out, "Each dollar spent on enforcing drug laws and fighting the violent crime these laws stimulate is a dollar that cannot be spent fighting other violent crime." Drug money corrupts law enforcement officials: a sting operation in the District of Columbia Police Department a few years ago sent a large number of officers to jail. Because participants in drug transactions do not report crimes to the police, officers often engage in nefarious tactics—urine testing, roadblocks, school locker searches, wiretaps, and racial "profiles"—to enforce the laws. Police coffers are swelled by the proceeds of property secured through "asset forfeiture"—usually without judicial process—which leads to outrageous abuses of private property rights and creates perverse economic incentives that have no place in objective law-enforcement decisions.[76]

Just as drugs have devastated minority inner-city communities, so have the laws that prohibit drugs. The artificially high profits entice new drug dealers. "A poorly educated young person in the inner city now has three choices: welfare, a low-wage job, or the glamorous and high-profit drug business," Ostrowski observes. "How can a teacher persuade students to study hard, when dropouts drive BMWs?" Talented entrepreneurs are drawn into the criminal world. In the process, notes Ostrowski, "[h]onesty, respect for private property, and other marks of a law-abiding community are further casualties of the drug laws." Nobel laureate Milton Friedman, a strong proponent of drug legalization, agrees: "Al Capone epitomizes our earlier attempt at Prohibition," he says. "[T]he Crips and Bloods epitomize this one."[77]

Drug legalization would remove most of the profit incentive to engage in the drug market, and would reduce substantially the involvement of organized crime. It would free up enormous police resources to more meritorious endeavors, and probably would reduce substantially the "secondary" crimes committed to support drug addictions. But realistically, legalization probably would lead to increased numbers of addicts, as the penalties (and stigma) associated with drug use diminish.

Is there a middle course? Drug abuse is unquestionably a legitimate government concern. But is it a criminal or a public health and safety matter? Could we maintain (or perhaps even elevate) the stigma against drug use, while treating abuse of currently illicit drugs as a health problem? Tobacco and alcohol inflict far more deaths and other social costs than illegal drugs, yet government goes so far as to subsidize tobacco, and treats alcohol as a criminal problem only when drinkers inflict harm upon others or drive while intoxicated.

Drug policy presents a difficult conundrum, but it appears that the costs of the war on drugs vastly outweigh its benefits—and that no possible law-enforcement expenditure will curb the drug market. For that reason, reasonable voices are increasingly calling current policies into question. In 1997, a group of thirty-four scientists, drug policy experts, and public officials—including former New York City police commissioner William Bratton and social scientist John DiIulio, Jr.—signed a statement saying that many current drug policies have done more harm than good and calling for consideration of alternatives. "The current drug-policy debate is marked by polarization into two positions stereotyped as 'drug warrior' and 'legalizer,'" the signers declared. "This creates the false impression that 'ending prohibition' is the only alternative to an unrestricted 'war on drugs,' effectively disenfranchising citizens who find both of those options unsatisfactory."[78]

The statement declares that current drug policies are not a prudent use of public funds or scarce prison capacity. It urges that drug policies should be judged by their results, not their intentions; that social disapproval, while a powerful deterrent to drug use, should not breed indiscriminate hostility to drug users; that drug users who violate the rights of others while under the influence of drugs or while trying to obtain them should be held responsible; and that policies should be tailored to different drugs based on risks and patterns of use. "A lot of politicians have avoided talking about drug policy because there is no articulated middle ground," asserts one of the signers, University of California psychologist Robert MacCoun. "We want to make clear to them that there's a whole palette of choices, and any criticism of the status quo doesn't have to imply endorsement of drug use."[79]

Passage of initiatives in California and Arizona legalizing medicinal use of marijuana suggests a possible moderation in public attitudes toward certain drug usage—but the dug-in resistance to those initiatives also demonstrates the tenacity of defenders of the status quo. In perhaps no other area of public policy is it so politically unacceptable to question the exorbitant costs and paltry benefits of current policies. We seriously need to reconsider the criminalization of drugs; but at the same time, advocates of drug legalization need to acknowledge that public support for their position simply does not exist. Statesmanship, not political demagoguery, is necessary to address the very real drug problem in this country.

When William J. Bennett resigned as drug czar, he remarked, "Give me stronger families, stronger churches and stronger schools, and I will give you back 90 percent of this problem."[80] Bennett was right—and not just about drugs, but about crime in general. For ultimately, the only enduring solutions to crime must come from communities themselves. As James Q. Wilson observes, "A free society depends on the conscience and reputations of individuals and the social norms of communities to maintain order. That is what has collapsed in America."[81]

We must rebuild those social norms. Public policy alone is insufficient. But public policies that support positive social norms—and that deliver power into the hands of those with the greatest incentive to preserve the rule of law—can't come quickly enough.

ACTION PROPOSALS

1. *Reestablish freedom from crime as a civil right.* The rule of law is essential to a free society, but is has eroded dangerously. Personal security once ranked highest in the civil rights movement's lexicon of values, but lately it has all but disappeared in favor of criminals' rights. In a free society, law enforcement must recognize the boundaries of individual liberty, boundaries that in our nation are defined in the Bill of Rights. But freedom is impossible if people fear predation from others. Enforcing the rule of law so people may enjoy the blessings of freedom should once again be the first object of government, and efforts toward that end should be directed to where erosion of the rule of law is greatest: inner cities.

2. *Color-blind justice.* In order to maintain popular support among all citizens, law enforcement must be blind to color. Toward that end, the costs in terms of the justifiable resentment and alienation caused by the use of race in criminal profiles outweigh any possible benefits. Racial profiles should be forbidden by federal law, pursuant to congressional authority to enforce the Fourteenth Amendment. Other official uses of race, such as race-based challenges to jurors, also should not be tolerated by courts.

3. *Quality of life.* Laws protecting people and property should be vigorously enforced. Graffiti, vandalism, auto theft, menacing public behavior—too often those crimes are ignored by law enforcement authorities. But their proliferation produces a sense of moral decay and lawlessness that leads to greater crimes. Police should give greater attention to crimes that erode quality of life.

4. *Community policing.* Rather than employing mercenary police forces and merely responding to crimes, law enforcement should be community-oriented and preventative in its focus. That means an active and ongoing presence in communities and constant interaction with citizens, including neighborhood substations, increased use of foot patrols, and community anticrime organizing.

5. *Serious penalties for crimes against people and property.* Strict enforcement of laws protecting people and their property has a strong deterrent effect—mainly by keeping criminals off the streets—and sends a strong signal that such crimes will not be tolerated. So long as due-process mechanisms are in place to ensure that individuals are treated fairly in the criminal-justice process, statistics showing "disproportionate" effects of law enforcement should not form a basis for excusing criminal behavior.

6. *Reduce abuses of asset forfeiture power.* Allowing police to seize assets involved in crimes without due process of law and to keep financial proceeds from their sale have the effects of violating the rights of innocent people and of distorting police priorities. Law enforcement discretion and limited police resources should not be driven by financial gain. Congress should enact strict limits on the asset forfeiture power and remove financial incentives, possibly by steering proceeds into victim restitution rather than letting them fill police coffers.

7. *Devolve law enforcement and criminal prosecution to the community level.* Community support of law enforcement is vital to preserving respect for the rule of law, and law enforcement is more effective when those who wield it have a direct stake in the community. For those reasons, we should explore devolution of law enforcement to the community level. That means breaking up large police departments and prosecutor offices and placing control in the hands of the community, with the power and resources to enforce community norms and priorities. Central

police offices should provide support and ensure that community law-enforcement authorities are free from corruption. In all other respects, authority and accountability should be invested in community law enforcement.

8. *Private security.* Economically disadvantaged communities, including public housing communities, should be given greater power to engage private security. Governmental entities could contract with community organizations to provide such services or provide block grants so communities could arrange for private security.

9. *Youth intervention.* Given the explosive growth in juvenile crimes, greater emphasis should be placed on juvenile criminals and young people who are at risk of engaging in crime. Public officials should employ community organizations to monitor, mentor, and minister to young people to break the spiral of criminality. Courts should consider out-placement of at-risk youths—through termination of parental rights, institutional placements, or referrals to community organizations—rather than keeping them in crime-ridden environments. Private school placements for at-risk youths should be an option for parents, courts, and education officials.

10. *Victims' rights.* The emphasis on victims of crimes should be restored to our criminal justice system. Through state and federal legislation or constitutional amendments, victims should be accorded enforceable rights to participate meaningfully in the criminal-justice process and to receive restitution from the criminal to the fullest practicable extent.

11. *Reconsider drug laws.* We should carefully examine the costs and benefits of drug laws and consider alternatives, such as treating drugs primarily as a serious health and safety problem and criminalizing only the abuse of drugs that leads to harm to others. Here and elsewhere, we should recognize that an enduring rule of law relies not on the maintenance of a police state, but on high moral standards internalized by the people.

7

EMPOWERMENT, POLITICS, AND FREEDOM

Our goal is freedom. I believe we will win it because the goal of the nation is freedom.

—Rev. Martin Luther King, Jr.[1]

For the vast majority of Americans, the problems discussed in this book have little direct impact. Relatively few Americans are touched by violent crime, chronic joblessness, welfare dependency, or abysmal schools. True, some of those problems—particularly out-of-wedlock births and declining public schools—are encroaching into hitherto safe suburban havens; but by and large, the vast majority of Americans are busy pursuing their own dreams. When they think about poor inner-city people at all, it is with a mixture of curiosity and disdain—and assuredly from a safe distance. Why should those Americans concern themselves with people they likely never will meet, with whom they perceive little in common, and whose problems are utterly alien to them?

There are lots of possible reasons, ranging from the charitable impulse to liberal guilt to growing tax burdens. But no reason is more important or urgent than this: the freedom of one American is inextricably bound up with the freedom of every other American. When one person is deprived of freedom, the freedom of every other person is compromised, for the rules that protect freedom are weakened by every deprivation or exception.

The founders of the American experiment understood that fact. That is why they guaranteed all Americans fundamental individual rights, secured by the guarantee of equality under law—what Thomas Paine called "this broad base, this universal foundation, that gives security to all and every part of society." For, explained Paine, "where the rights of man are equal, every man must finally see the necessity of protecting the rights of others as the most effectual security for his own."[2] A century later, as recently emancipated blacks encountered the oppression of the Jim Crow regime, Booker T. Washington made the same point in this warning:

> We shall constitute one-third and more of the ignorance and crime of the South, or one-third of its intelligence and progress; we shall contribute one-third to the business and industrial prosperity of the South, or we shall prove a veritable body of death, stagnating, depressing, retarding every effort to advance the body politic.[3]

Washington was prescient: every time we have denied any of our citizens fundamental freedoms or equality under law, we have all paid dearly for it. Today, we have a massive, costly, and debilitating welfare state, a divisive regime of racial classifications and preferences, and attendant social pathologies because too often our nation has failed to honor its guarantees of equal rights for all Americans. We have denied, and continue to deny, basic opportunities to many of our citizens: the opportunity to obtain educational opportunities, to earn an honest living, to walk safe streets. We face today the same choice we always have had: either we can make good on the promise of opportunity, or we can continue—all of us—to pay the price.

The preceding chapters have outlined concrete ways in which America can finally fulfill the promise of opportunity. The question remains: is our political process, so often dominated by special-interest groups battling over entitlements, capable of empowering the least-fortunate members of society so that all of us can enjoy greater freedom?

As we approach the millennium, it seems clear that increasingly, Americans define themselves politically not in terms of partisan affiliations, class, or even race, but in terms of their relationship with government. Those who depend upon the state for their sustenance support political parties and candidates who promise to expand the scope of government and the regulatory welfare state; those who rely on themselves favor parties and candidates who promise greater freedom to do so.

I remember a few years again when my client and friend, Taalib-din Uqdah, decided to run for the City Council in Washington, D.C. A charismatic man with strong business and philanthropic community ties, Uqdah ran on an empowerment platform, supporting government reform and efficiency, more private sector job opportunities, and school choice. He was trounced. "What I didn't realize until I started campaigning," he told me, "is that 80 percent of the people in the District either work for the city or are dependent on someone who does." Uqdah had discovered how powerful interests, with patronage and the coercive apparatus of government at their disposal, conspire to preserve the status quo, whatever the cost. Observes Fred Siegel, "Social services have become both big business and the key to a politics that revolves around serving and expanding the social service industry."[4]

We did not arrive where we are today by accident. For generations, the political left has understood that the surest means to accomplish its redistributionist agenda is to make people more dependent on the state. Starting with the New Deal, and hastening with the Great Society, the left has worked methodically to expand the role and scope of government. In *The Future Once Happened Here*, Fred Siegel describes the ideology and tactics of the activists who dramatically expanded the welfare state during the 1960s and 1970s. The crucial first step, as antipoverty activist Richard Elman explained in 1966, was to "make dependency legitimate." According to Elman, all people were dependent on social structures that arranged benefits and burdens, but the poor were disadvantaged by those arrangements. "We must try to create even more agencies of dependency," announced Elman, "and we must make it possible for all to make use of them equally."[5]

The "vehicle for Elman's transvaluation of values," Siegel recounts, was "the marriage of antipoverty and civil rights law."[6] The Legal Aid Society (our tax dollars at work) pushed for a judicially created "right" to welfare, and the liberal courts obliged. The welfare advocates understood that the new economic incentives would undermine traditional institutions and lead to demands for ever-increasing entitlements. The welfare state obtained a huge new constituency, but at tremendous cost. "In the name of antipoverty," declares Siegel, the welfare revolution "trapped people in dependency."[7]

Several decades later, the welfare state is collapsing under its own weight, yet the crusade to expand government continues. The epochal defeat of nationalized health care led President Clinton to declare that the era of big government is over. But the administration merely shifted gears, moving incrementally yet relentlessly to expand the constituency of government. Apart from its acquiescence in welfare reform, all of the administration's domestic policies—whether Americorps, federally subsidized child care, or expanded Medicare and federal child health benefits—promise to expand the scope and role of government in people's lives.

Too often, Republicans and conservatives respond not with principled opposition or deregulatory alternatives, but with scaled-down versions of welfare-state schemes. If Democrats propose some new entitlement, Republicans come up with their own versions. At that point the battle is lost, for the question is no longer whether government's power will expand, but only how much and how fast. That strategy—what I call preemptive capitulation—typically fails not only as policy but as politics, for those voters who favor government expansion will gravitate toward their real champions rather than a pale imitation.[8] Yet the pattern repeats itself time and again.

The modern conservative politician who best understood those dynamics and how to change them was Margaret Thatcher, and her lessons are instructive for advocates of freedom. When Thatcher became prime minister of Great Britain in 1979, she was faced with circumstances far more dire than in America today. Huge portions of the economy were in state hands, mired in inefficiency and labor strife. Labor unions and large corporations controlled the government through negotiations over beer and sandwiches at No. 10 Downing

Street. The unions wreaked havoc through strikes and violence, often bringing major services to a standstill. Taxes were confiscatory, prosperity was declining. People were dependent on the state for their jobs, housing, and health care—and therefore were heavily invested in expanding government's resources and power.[9]

But because conditions had grown so bad, a growing number of citizens were willing to give someone new a chance. Thatcher came to power with a clear philosophy that directly challenged the status quo:

> Let me give you my vision: a man's right to work as he will, to spend what he earns, to own property, to have the state as servant and not as master: these are the British inheritance. They are the essence of a free country, and on that freedom all our other freedoms depend.[10]

Thatcher set out to fundamentally change the relationship between the people and the state. She started by slashing taxes, thereby allowing individuals rather than government to decide how to spend their money. She also determined to restore the rule of law, curbing the disruptive and coercive powers of labor unions and restoring social stability.

Thatcher pursued a multifaceted agenda of individual empowerment. Its cornerstone was "popular capitalism," which consisted of privatizing government-owned corporations. She also privatized public housing, creating tens of thousands of new property owners, and provided low-income families the means to opt out of government schools. Special interests with a powerful stake in the status quo resisted the reforms tenaciously, whereas popular support was diffused. But Thatcher persisted, and once the programs were in place, she achieved political transformation: as people began to look to the private sector for their incomes and became shareholders and homeowners, they gained a powerful ownership stake in free enterprise and private property, fueling Britain's transition from socialism to capitalism. They voted accordingly: Conservatives outpolled the Labor Party among first-time buyers of shares in newly privatized companies by a margin of 53 to 14 percent.

The transformation was fundamental and enduring, so that going back to the days of socialism was impossible. Not only was Thatcher elected to three terms—and her Conservative successor, John Major, to another—even after Labor won control again, Prime Minister Tony Blair has pressed forward on several fronts, particularly welfare reform.[11]

We need, it seems to me, a Thatcherite empowerment strategy in America. The challenge is to create—through economic liberty, private-sector education alternatives, private property ownership, and so on—a tangible stake in freedom for those who are dependent on the government. Those who favor bigger government always enjoy the short-term advantage, for their strategy lavishes immediate material benefits—whether welfare, health care, or affirmative action. Freedom offers only potential; but therein lies its advantage, for while the welfare state must ultimately collapse under its own weight, the potential for freedom is limitless. Our task is to illustrate, vividly and tangibly, the real-world human benefits of freedom to people who have been most denied it.

That means bringing the fight to new frontiers: to the inner cities, and to minorities and the poor. Opportunities to do so abound. Social engineering and wealth redistribution have failed miserably. And as the columnist William Raspberry acknowledges, liberals "haven't had a bright new idea in ages. . . . It is mostly the conservatives who have got us rethinking welfare, public education, racial fairness, the size and reach of government—even the role of philanthropy and charity."[12] With regard to many of those ideas, liberals are simply too hemmed in by their attachments to special-interest alliances—particularly labor unions and government bureaucrats—to be able to respond effectively. That gives pragmatic, forward-thinking conservatives and libertarians huge logistical advantages.

Moreover, as discussed in chapter 2, polls suggest that minorities and the poor are far more conservative and traditional in their philosophy and values than most of the leaders who purport to speak for them. Robert Woodson puts it bluntly: "We need to stop celebrating those who define us as victims." To break the liberal vise grip, says Woodson, "A first and critical step is to establish what should be a natural alliance between conservatives and low-income Americans who, consistently, when surveyed, have registered their support for conservative values and principles."[13] Emanuel Little, publisher of *Destiny* magazine, agrees. "There are rumblings in the black community that most outsiders cannot see or feel," he reports. "While white viewers listen to Jesse Jackson rant on TV, black people are sitting in front of their own TVs saying, 'This guy's got to be kidding!'"[14]

George Mason University economics professor Walter Williams sounds a cautionary note: "[E]ven though blacks register conservative attitudes across the board, they will still say they're not Republican or conservative. There's a stigma that's associated with these labels in the black community."[15] I remember State Representative Polly Williams, with whom I worked closely on the Milwaukee school choice litigation, making a similar point. "The liberals say they want to help us, but the one thing they won't do is let us control our own lives. Conservatives don't give a damn about us, but the one thing they're willing to do is to give us the keys." She paused for a moment, then added, "I think I'm beginning to like conservatives better."

Not everyone shares Polly Williams' pragmatism, and the fact is that through their not-so-benign neglect of the concerns of minorities and the poor, conservatives have earned themselves a huge dose of cynicism among many minority Americans. Furthermore, even as they indicate conservative views on many social and political issues, most minorities typically believe the government should play a central role in providing opportunities. "The black middle class cannot be compared with some white suburban group because they didn't get there by the same means," observes Elizabeth Wright, publisher of the insightful journal *Issues and Views*. Many successful blacks are employed by government or are beneficiaries of affirmative action. Says Wright, "They feel constantly unstable, fearful that it's all going to be taken away from them."[16] And yet, many are dissatisfied with the schools and economic opportunities that the government provides.

Overall, the terrain presents unique opportunities—and difficult challenges—for conservatives. Says Woodson, "If conservatism is to become a viable movement with sustained and substantial impact, the thinking of those on the right must move beyond ideological jousts with the left to an honest internal self-evaluation."[17] Conservatives and libertarians must decide that they care about those who have been excluded from the American Dream. And they must demonstrate convincingly that the interests of minorities and the urban poor lie not with government programs but with free enterprise, educational choice, and the like.

Republicans have the most to gain, and the most to lose. As Stephan and Abigail Thernstrom point out, if the huge Democratic edge in black votes had been negated, Republicans would have won every presidential election since 1968.[18] Shifting racial demographics make it a necessity for the party to broaden its base: the percentage of Americans who are white will decline from about 74 percent today to 67 percent by the year 2010.[19] But Republicans have not done well among most minority voters. Since 1980, Republican presidential candidates have received a consistently paltry 11 to 12 percent of black votes.[20] Meanwhile, the Republican share of Hispanic votes declined from 37 percent in 1984 to 30 percent in 1988 and 25 percent in 1992, despite deeply held conservative values among many Hispanics. The percentage of Hispanics voting Republican is shrinking as the number of Hispanic voters in the electorate is growing.[21] At the same time, the percentage of low-income voters supporting Republican presidential candidates also has plummeted: in 1984, Ronald Reagan received a remarkable 45 percent of votes from voters with incomes below $15,000, but the GOP share dropped to 37 percent in 1988 and to 23 percent in 1992.[22] That decline suggests that poor Americans increasingly are disinclined to view Republicans as the party of opportunity.

The Joint Center for Political and Economic Studies consistently finds that roughly one-third of blacks identify themselves as conservative—but only about 5 percent identify themselves as Republican.[23] That huge variation—5 percent versus 33 percent—represents an opportunity gap for Republicans: even if the GOP were unable to reach self-described "moderates," at least it should be able to attract conservative blacks. The fact that, consistently, it has not demonstrates the skepticism, if not outright contempt, with which many black Americans view the party that once they supported overwhelmingly.

How can Republicans close that gap? First, by making the effort. Republicans often write off minority voters, or talk to minority voters about issues perceived as peculiarly of concern to minorities. If the preceding chapters demonstrate anything, it is that Americans of all races share common concerns. If Republicans were to take their message of freedom and opportunity to black and Hispanic schools and churches, they might be pleasantly surprised by their reception.

Republicans also can succeed by presenting themselves as something other than a warmed-over version of Democrats. Some Republicans, such as former New Jersey Governor Thomas Kean, have succeeded among black voters by embracing affirmative action and other liberal programs. But others, such as former President George Bush, have failed to attract black voters with liberal pabulum. Current New Jersey Governor Christine Whitman, for instance, won 25 percent of the black vote in her first election, but slipped to about 10 percent in 1997.[24] Whitman supported affirmative action, but did nothing to empower low-income people in the inner cities. By contrast, New York City Mayor Rudy Giuliani, running on a solid record of empowerment, increased his percentage of black support from 5 percent in 1993 to 20 percent four years later.[25] Likewise, Los Angeles Mayor Richard Riordan, stressing a platform of economic and entrepreneurial opportunities, increased his share of the Hispanic vote from 43 percent in 1993 to 60 percent in 1997.[26]

For whatever reason, Republicans seem to follow instinctively the Bush-Whitman model of patrician paternalism over the Giuliani model of empowerment. Many Republicans are afraid to oppose racial preferences for fear they will alienate minority voters. Ironically, the California Civil Rights Initiative—despite being opposed bitterly by establishment civil rights groups—won about 26 percent of black votes, outpolling GOP presidential candidate Bob Dole by more than 2 to 1 among black voters.

All of these statistics suggest that black voters are more likely to support a candidate who stands for something over someone who stands for nothing. More significant, traditional Republican values—individual initiative, free enterprise, safe streets—can have powerful appeal among minority voters.

A good model for this strategy is Mayor Giuliani, who preaches the same political sermon whether his audience is white, black, or Hispanic. His focus on reducing crime and improving the quality of life won favor not only from whites but minority voters as well: 50 percent of blacks gave the mayor high marks on the crime issue, along with 60 percent of Hispanics and 83 percent of whites.[27] Not only did Giuliani quadruple his share of the black vote, but he also improved his showing among

Hispanic voters from 37 percent in 1993 to 43 percent in 1997. "The fact is the change in the minority vote created a difference between a narrow victory and a very large one," the mayor remarked.[28]

Skeptics may attribute Giuliani's success to his generally moderate politics, but more conservative Republicans also have reaped success among minority voters by aggressively pursuing empowerment policies. In a city where only 6 percent of the voters are Republicans, Jersey City's Mayor Bret Schundler won 40 percent of the black vote and 60 percent of the Hispanic vote, despite Jesse Jackson's active opposition.[29] Indianapolis Mayor Stephen Goldsmith also has attracted large numbers of black supporters.

Unquestionably the most effective Republican, on both the politics and policy of empowerment, is Wisconsin Governor Tommy Thompson. A quick study and a relentless campaigner, over three terms Thompson has made himself no stranger to inner-city Milwaukee. He first pushed his Learnfare program, linking welfare benefits to children's school attendance. Then he ushered through the nation's first school voucher program, allowing hundreds—and later, thousands—of economically disadvantaged children to leave failing public schools for excellent community private schools chosen by their parents. The crescendo was the nation's most sweeping welfare reform law, combining stringent work requirements with generous child-care and health-care benefits. Through it all, he has brought his case to the people who are most affected, wielding popular support against intransigent opposition from unions and other powerful interest groups. "You have to have a lot of stamina," Thompson observes.[30] Nor has he slowed the pace: as his third term nears its end, Thompson continues to blaze new frontiers. He has proposed a state takeover of the Milwaukee Public Schools in three years unless the district improves dramatically its students' test scores and graduation and attendance rates. He also supports refundable tax credits for elementary and secondary education expenses, among other reforms. The governor's bold initiatives have not only expanded opportunities for Wisconsin's poorest citizens, but also earned political dividends: Thompson carried 40 percent of the state's black voters in his bid for a third term in 1994.[31] The lessons: good policies make good politics, and elected officials who reinvest their political capital in giving power to the people can reap huge rewards. As William Bennett comments in the context of Thompson's welfare reform program,

> We *are* the compassionate party, because this is compassionate policy. This policy is saving lives. It is saving children. It is putting people in a position to hold their heads high and take responsibility for their own lives. This is *true* compassion. It's tough love, yes. It's hard-headed, but it is compassion as we were always taught—having a soft heart and a hard head. That's a very good combination, and it describes what Governor Thompson has done.[32]

Tommy Thompson's direction is exactly where Republicans need to head. Jesse Jackson aptly has remarked, "[T]he best way to move people is through enlightened self-interest."[33] If Republicans go into the inner cities and offer safe streets, community renewal, and real economic and educational opportunities, there is little the Democrats can do to compete. Nothing, for instance, is more important to most mothers than their children's education. The idea of school choice—giving low-income families the chance to enroll their children in good, safe schools—resonates powerfully. And Democrats—unless they are willing to forsake their most influential supporters, the teacher unions—cannot possibly offer anything so tangible. Indeed, school choice draws strongest support, by far, from blacks and Hispanics.[34] Yet liberals are openly patronizing and disdainful. "It's exploitative of the black community," sniffs Mary Jean Collins, national field director of People for the American Way, which has suckered the National Association for the Advancement of Colored People into an alliance opposing school choice. "The philosophy of the right is always, 'Give my kid what he wants and to hell with the rest.' For that attitude to get into the black community would be shameful."[35]

What is shameful is the open contempt that liberals show for individual empowerment, and unquestionably that creates opportunities for nontraditional alliances. For empowerment transcends the partisan and ideological divides. The major empowerment triumphs—from school choice to welfare reform—have occurred mostly through alliances between conservative Republicans, moderate Democrats, and progressive black officials: Wisconsin Governor Tommy Thompson and State Representative Polly Williams teamed up on school choice in Milwaukee; Governor George Voinovich and Councilwoman Fannie Lewis on school choice in Cleveland; Governor Thompson, State Representative Antonio Riley, and Mayor John Norquist's chief of staff, David Riemer, on welfare reform in Wisconsin. On school choice for the District of Columbia, which received majority votes in both the U.S. Senate and House of Representatives but died by filibuster, chief supporters were Senator Joseph Lieberman (D-CT), Representative Dick Armey (R-TX), and Rep. Floyd Flake (D-NY). Black Virginia legislators join forces frequently with conservatives on social issues such as parental rights.[36]

Much of the action on empowerment is pushed by a bold new generation of mayors, spanning both parties. Once upon a time it was quipped that the definition of a conservative was a liberal who had been mugged; today it might be said that a conservative is a liberal who was elected mayor of a big city. After years of corruption, inefficiency, and decay, some cities are reviving through the aggressive efforts of mayors committed to busting special-interest dominance, privatizing city services, and returning the streets to law-abiding citizens.

Rudy Giuliani is the best-known of the new breed, but other trailblazers include Democratic Mayors John Norquist of Milwaukee, Edward Rendell of Philadelphia, and Mark White of Cleveland; along with Republican Mayors Stephen Goldsmith of Indianapolis, Richard Riordan of Los Angeles, Bret Schundler of Jersey City, and Tom Fetzer of Raleigh. All have broken the mold of the big-city pols of yesteryear. Milwaukee's Norquist, a staunch advocate of school choice, complains that "[w]hat we have is a school-finance monopoly that is not helping public school children, is suppressing quality, is not customer-oriented, and is overly bureaucratic."[37] Riordan has devoted his second term to education reform. "We need revolution now," he says. "We cannot ask a parent to wait five to ten more years for the federal government to test their kids and find out they've failed. It is evil to ask a parent to send a child to a school that is a disaster."[38] Goldsmith has pushed contracting out city services, such as street-sweeping and park maintenance, to neighborhood groups and community-based businesses. "We tax somebody in a poor neighborhood, we accumulate their limited wealth, and then we hire somebody in another

neighborhood . . . to go back into the first neighborhood,"
Goldsmith declares. "It's not fair. It's not equitable."[39]

The exemplar of empowerment politics is the Rev. Floyd Flake, who
retired from Congress in 1997 midway through his sixth term to devote
more time to supporting school choice and developing enterprises in his
Jamaica, Queens community. In twenty-one years as pastor of Allen
African Methodist Episcopal Church, he has built an enormous congre-
gation, established a thriving private school with 480 pupils, transformed
vacant lots into homes, and fostered new businesses. As the *Washington
Post* describes Flake's politics, "Democrats are too beholden to special
interest groups, particularly unions, Flake argues. And most black leaders
are mired in the protest politics of the civil rights era and wasting precious
energy advocating welfare, affirmative action and other government
programs." Such efforts haven't helped those who need help the most.
"[O]ur communities still look like war zones," Flake says.[40] And priorities
are confused. "When a white person kills a black person, we all go out in
the street to protest," he observes. "But our children are being educationally killed every day in public schools and nobody says a thing."[41]

In Congress, Flake sponsored school choice legislation and the
American Community Renewal Act, while back in New York he
endorsed Mayor Giuliani's reelection. "I am beyond race and party
now," he remarked. Flake's refusal to remain in an ideological "box"
epitomizes the thinking necessary for empowerment to succeed: "The
reason we are not blessed," he argues, "is because we are living in a new
age but we are trying to do the same stuff that we did in the old days.
We're still acting like it's 1967 when it's now 1997. It's time for us to
do some growing up."[42]

That advice goes not only for liberals but for conservatives as well.
The first step is to care, the second is to act. "Unless we conservatives
get more involved in putting our ideas into action, into rolling up our
sleeves and getting involved, we will have failed our country and failed
those in need," declares David Kuo, executive director of the American
Compass. "The perverse incentives that rewarded illegitimacy and dis-
couraged work have been dramatically scaled back. States and cities have
unprecedented freedom to craft reforms. Now it is our responsibility—
and our opportunity."[43]

The Bradley Foundation's Michael S. Joyce provides this sage prescription: "[C]onservatism must reach beyond its traditional base in the suburban middle class and summon to its banner grass-roots, neighborhood leaders," he urges. "This would be the making of a new conservative majority—one that reaches across the racial and cultural divides that liberalism continues to emphasize and exacerbate—a majority united in the faith that, beneath our differences, we are all self-governing citizens of a republic committed to the notion that, here, the people rule."[44]

That unprecedented opportunity exists at this point in time partly because conditions for many are so bad, partly because grandiose solutions have failed—but also because we have always known the real solutions. America has become the greatest nation on earth because of our freedom. Here we have no guarantees, only possibilities, but they are endless. They are what people make of them.

Empowerment is about providing all Americans the opportunities that are their birthright. Empowerment is about giving a greater security to all our freedoms, which will come when all individuals—white and black, rich and poor—have a direct stake in preserving them.

We have put slavery, Communism, Jim Crow, and the welfare state behind us. Now is the time, at last, to get on with the unfinished business of making good on the promise of opportunity for all Americans.

NOTES

INTRODUCTION: THE CHALLENGE OF EMPOWERMENT

1. Quoted in Martin Luther King, Jr., *Where Do We Go From Here: Chaos or Community?* (New York: Harper and Row, Publishers, 1967), p. 70.

2. For two excellent books outlining the libertarian philosophy, see David Boaz, *Libertarianism: A Primer* (New York: Free Press, 1997); and Charles Murray, *What It Means to Be a Libertarian: A Personal Interpretation* (New York: Broadway Books, 1997).

3. My previous books include *The Affirmative Action Fraud: Can We Restore the American Civil Rights Vision?* (Washington, D.C.: Cato Institute, 1995); *Grassroots Tyranny and the Limits of Federalism* (Washington, D.C.: Cato Institute, 1993); *Unfinished Business: A Civil Rights Strategy for America's Third Century* (San Francisco: Pacific Research Institute, 1990); and *Changing Course: Civil Rights at the Crossroads* (New Brunswick, N.J.: Transaction Books, 1988).

4. Terry M. Neal, "Ex-Lawmaker Refuses to Be Boxed In," *Washington Post* (January 10, 1998), p. A8.

5. Virginia L. Postrel and James K. Glassman, "'National Greatness' or Conservative Malaise?" *Wall Street Journal* (September 25, 1997).

6. William Kristol and David Brooks, "What Ails Conservatism," *Wall Street Journal* (September 15, 1997).

7. Ronald Brownstein, "Local Activism Shows Way to New Consensus on Local Activism in Inner Cities," *Los Angeles Times* (December 22, 1997).

8. Quoted in Rochelle Watson, "Robert Woodson's Conservative Prescription for Change," *Ethnic Newswatch* (January 31, 1995).

CHAPTER 1: GRIM REALITIES

1. As this book was going into publication, the Milton S. Eisenhower Foundation released a report following up on the 1968 Kerner Commission report, echoing many of the findings presented in this chapter. See, for example, Michael A. Fletcher, "Kerner

Prophecy on Race Relations Came True: Report Says That Despite Progress, Foundation Finds 'Separate and Unequal' Societies More Deeply Rooted," *Washington Post* (March 1, 1998), p. A6. For a response to the Eisenhower Foundation report, criticizing in particular its view that unequal conditions are attributable to racism, see Abigail and Stephan Thernstrom, "American Apartheid? Don't Believe It," *Wall Street Journal* (March 2, 1998).

2. Lecture by Hannah M. Hawkins, Heritage Foundation, Washington, D.C. (Feb. 26, 1997).

3. James Q. Wilson, "Two Nations," American Enterprise Institute 1997 Francis Boyer Lecture (December 4, 1997).

4. See Mickey Kaus, *The End of Equality.* (New York: Basic Books, 1992).

5. See William Julius Wilson, *The Truly Disadvantaged: The Inner City, the Underclass and Public Policy* (Chicago: University of Chicago Press, 1987).

6. Clint Bolick, *The Affirmative Action Fraud: Can We Restore the American Civil Rights Vision?* (Washington: Cato Institute, 1996), pp. 51–68.

7. Quoted in Rochelle Watson, "Robert Woodson's Conservative Prescription for Change," *About . . . Time Magazine* (January 31, 1995), p. 16.

8. Gunnar Myrdal, *An American Dilemma: The Negro Problem and American Democracy* (New York: Harper & Row, 1944).

9. Stephan Thernstrom and Abigail Thernstrom, *America in Black and White: One Nation, Indivisible* (New York: Simon & Schuster, 1997), p. 184.

10. Steven A. Holmes, "A Rose-Colored View of Race," *New York Times* (June 17, 1997), section 4, p. 4.

11. Stephan Thernstrom and Abigail Thernstrom, "We Have Overcome," *The New Republic* (October 13, 1997), p. 24.

12. Thernstrom and Thernstrom, *America in Black and White*, p. 183.

13. Ibid., p. 196.

14. Ibid., p. 197.

15. Ibid., pp. 190–91.

16. Ibid., p. 192.

17. Ibid., p. 445.

18. Ibid., p. 211.

19. Ibid., p. 218.

20. Thernstrom and Thernstrom, "We Have Overcome," p. 76.

21. Ibid., pp. 27–28.

22. Joel Achenbach, "The Trial's End, in Stark Black and White," *Washington Post* (September 30, 1995), p. A13.

23. Thernstrom and Thernstrom, "We Have Overcome," p. 24.

24. Paul M. Sniderman and Thomas Piazza, *The Scar of Race* (Cambridge, Mass.: Belknap Press of Harvard University Press, 1993), p. 103.

25. *The State of Black America 1994* (Washington, D.C.: National Urban League, 1994), p. 18.

26. Dennis Kelly, "Kids' Scores for Reading 'In Trouble,'" *USA Today* (April 28–30, 1995), p. 1A.

27. Pierre Thomas, "1 in 3 Black Men in Justice System," *Washington Post* (October 5, 1995), p. A1.

28. *The State of Black America 1994*, p. 19.

29. Stephen Buttry, "From Birth to Death, Racial Gap Persists," *Omaha World-Herald* (June 15, 1997), p. 1A.

30. William Julius Wilson, *When Work Disappears: The World of the New Urban Poor* (New York: Alfred A. Knopf, 1996), p. 195.

31. U.S. Census Bureau, "Poverty 1995," Table A.

32. Andrew Hacker, *Two Nations: Black and White, Separate, Hostile, Unequal* (New York: Charles Scribner's Sons, 1992), p. 103.

33. Wilson, *When Work Disappears*, p. 15.

34. Thernstrom and Thernstrom, *America in Black and White*, p. 207.

35. Wilson, *When Work Disappears*, p. 14.

36. Ibid., p. 11.

37. For a particularly insightful analysis, see Steven Hayward, "Broken Cities: Liberalism's Urban Legacy," *Policy Review* (March/April 1998), p. 14.

38. Wilson, *When Work Disappears*, p. 72.

39. Cited in Wilson, "Two Nations."

40. Thernstrom and Thernstrom, *America in Black and White*, p. 239.

41. Ibid., p. 240.

42. Ibid., p. 236.

43. Wilson, *When Work Disappears*, p. 92.

44. Patrick F. Fagan, "Social Breakdown in America" in Stuart Butler and Kim Holmes, eds., *Issues '96: The Candidate's Briefing Book* (Washington, D.C.: 1996). pp. 168–70.

45. "Vital Signs: Higher Education Equality Index," *Journal of Blacks in Higher Education* (June 30, 1995), p. 50.

46. Thernstrom and Thernstrom, *America in Black and White*, p. 192.

47. Ibid., p. 408. For instance, Harvard adds approximately 95 points to the average black Scholastic Aptitude Test score and has a 5 percent black dropout rate; Columbia adds 182 points and has a 25 percent black dropout rate; the University of California at Berkeley added (before the ban on preferential admissions policies) 288 points and had a 42 percent black dropout rate.

48. Thernstrom and Thernstrom, *America in Black and White*, p. 355.

49. Cheryl W. Thompson, "Young Blacks Entangled in Legal System," *Washington Post* (August 26, 1997), p. B1.

50. Wilson, *When Work Disappears*, p. 21.

51. Richard D. Kahlenberg, *The Remedy: Class, Race, and Affirmative Action* (New York: Basic Books, 1996), p. 45.

52. Katherine Kersten, "Affirmative Action Not the Answer," *Minneapolis Star Tribune* (June 25, 1997), p. 15A.

53. Office of the Press Secretary, The White House, "Remarks by the President in Outreach Meeting" (December 19, 1997).

54. Wilson, *When Work Disappears*, p. 197.

55. See Clint Bolick, *The Affirmative Action Fraud: Can We Restore the American Civil Rights Vision?*, pp. 51–68.

56. Wilson, *When Work Disappears*, p. 195.

57. Martin Luther King, Jr., "I Have a Dream," in James M. Washington, ed., *A Testament of Hope: The Essential Writings and Speeches of Martin Luther King, Jr.* (New York: HarperCollins, 1986), p. 217.

CHAPTER 2: BLACKS AND WHITES ON COMMON GROUND

1. Quoted in Richard H. King, *Civil Rights and the Idea of Freedom* (New York: Oxford University Press, 1992), p. 13.

2. Gunnar Myrdal, *An American Dilemma* (New York: Harper and Brothers Publishers, 1944), p. 4.

3. See Bolick, *The Affirmative Action Fraud*, pp. 23–38.

4. See Clint Bolick, "Everlasting King," *Reason* (July 1991), pp. 52–54.

5. William Julius Wilson, *When Work Disappears: The World of the New Urban Poor* (New York: Alfred A. Knopf, 1996), p. 67.

6. Michael F. Frisby, "White House Reworks a Troubled Race Initiative as President Heads to a Town Meeting in Ohio," *Wall Street Journal* (December 3, 1997), p. A24.

7. Cinqué Henderson, "Myths of the Unloved," *The New Republic* (August 25, 1997), p. 15.

8. Thernstrom and Thernstrom, *America in Black and White*, p. 303.

9. Paul Gigot, "GOP Confronts Future Without Hispanics: Adios?" *Wall Street Journal* (August 22, 1997).

10. Survey conducted from November 5–7, 1996, by the Polling Company, Washington D.C.

11. Reported in Clint Bolick, "Blacks and Whites on Common Ground," *Wall Street Journal* (August 5, 1992).

12. Michael A. Fletcher, "Low-Profile Year 'Extremely Productive' for NAACP, Mfume Says," *Washington Post* (February 16, 1997), p. A3.

13. David A. Bositis, *1997 National Opinion Poll: Children's Issues* (Washington, D.C.: Joint Center for Political and Economic Studies, 1997), p. 4.

14. *Differences in Black and White Opinion on Important Issues of Public Policy* (Washington, D.C.: Center for New Black Leadership, 1996), p. 8.

15. Reported in Watson, "Robert Woodson's Conservative Prescription for Change."

16. Thernstrom and Thernstrom, *America in Black and White*, pp. 303–304.

17. *Differences in Black and White Opinion*, pp. 15–16 and 31.

18. Bositis, *1997 National Opinion Poll: Children's Issues*, Table 5.

19. Ibid., Table 7. See also Joe Williams, "Blacks Increasingly Support School Choice, Poll Says," *Milwaukee Journal Sentinel* (July 28, 1997).

20. See Elena Neuman, "Color Them Conservative: Beliefs of Blacks Belie Their Politics," *Washington Times* (October 20, 1993), p. A13.

21. Reported in Bolick, "Blacks and Whites on Common Ground."

22. For a superb article on this issue, see Glenn Garvin, "Loco, Completamente Loco," *Reason* (January 1998), p. 18.

23. Fletcher, "Low-Profile Year," p. A3.

24. Ibid., p. A3.

25. Thernstrom and Thernstrom, *America in Black and White*, p. 304.

26. *Differences in Black and White Opinion*, pp. 4–7 and 20–22.

27. See Paul M. Sniderman and Thomas Piazza, *The Scar of Race* (Cambridge, Mass.: Belknap Press of Harvard University Press, 1993).

28. Sam Howe Verhovek, "In Poll, Americans Reject Means But Not Ends of Racial Diversity," *New York Times* (December 14, 1997).

29. Verhovek, "Poll."

30. David A. Bositis, *1997 National Opinion Poll: Race Relations* (Washington, D.C.: Joint Center for Political and Economic Studies, 1997), Table 9.

31. Verhovek, "Poll."

32. See Bolick, *The Affirmative Action Fraud*, pp. 126 and 159 n.9.

33. Verhovek, "Poll." An argument for socioeconomic affirmative action is presented in Richard D. Kahlenberg, *The Remedy: Class, Race, and Affirmative Action* (New York: Basic Books, 1996).

34. I squared off with Abigail Thernstrom, a member of the Institute for Justice Board of Directors and a scholar whom I admire intensely, on this very issue. See "Racial Affirmative Action Is on the Way Out. Should Income-Based Preferences Replace It? Clint Bolick and Abigail Thernstrom Have Two Views," *The American Enterprise* (July/August 1995).

35. U.S. Bureau of the Census, Poverty 1995: Graphs.

36. Ibid., Table A.

37. Donald Lambro, "Set-Aside Disfavor Crosses Party Lines," *Washington Times* (November 13, 1997), p. A8.

38. Sniderman and Piazza, *The Scar of Race*, pp. 35–87.

39. Randall Kennedy, "My Race Problem—And Ours," *Atlantic Monthly* (May 1997).

40. Wilson, *When Work Disappears*, p. 181.

CHAPTER 3: THE EDUCATION IMPERATIVE

1. Affidavit of Pilar Gonzalez, *Jackson v. Benson*, July 25, 1995.

2. Sheryl Stolberg, "Dreamers, Doubters, Survivors," *Los Angeles Times* (June 30, 1996), p. A1.

3. Ibid.

4. Charles Murray, *Losing Ground* (New York: Basic Books, 1984), p. 105.

5. Dennis Kelly, "Kids' Scores for Reading 'In Trouble,'" *USA Today* (April 28–30, 1995), p. 1A.

6. "U.S. Students Make Progress in Math," *Dallas Morning News* (February 28, 1997), p. 6A.

7. Robert M. Huelskamp, "Perspectives on Education in America," *Phi Delta Kappan* (May 1993), p. 719. Within an article that paints an excessively rosy overall picture of American education, the author cannot escape the fact that the system is failing large numbers of minority children.

8. Jake Thompson, "Jackson Calls Nation's Attention to Its Educational 'Emergency,'" *Kansas City Star* (Feb. 22, 1997), p. A1.

9. From a study by Arthur Hauptman and Maureen McLaughlin, "Is the Goal of College Access Being Met?" quoted in Nancy Hoffman, "Shifting Gears: How to Get Results with Affirmative Action," *Change* (March/April 1993), p. 31.

10. Hoffman, "Shifting Gears," p. 31.

11. Quoted in Hoffman, "Shifting Gears," p. 32.

12. *Hopwood v. Texas*, 78 F.3d 932 (5th Cir.), *cert. denied*, 116 S.Ct. 2850 (1996).

13. See David J. Armor, *Forced Justice: School Desegregation and the Law* (New York: Oxford University Press, 1995); Bolick, *The Affirmative Action Fraud*, pp. 75–76.

14. Sol Stern, "The Invisible Miracle of Catholic Schools," *City Journal* (Summer 1996), p. 14.

15. Chester E. Finn, Jr., "Learning-Free Zones," *Policy Review* (September/October 1997), pp. 34–38.

16. When I first toured low-income neighborhoods in Milwaukee in 1990 with State Rep. Polly Williams and her aide, Larry Harwell, I pointed out a well-manicured public school that stood out in stark contrast to most of the dilapidated public schools we had driven past. "Oh, that's a 'magnet' school," Rep. Williams explained. "It brings in white kids from the suburbs. None of our kids get to go there."

17. Nina H. Shokraii, "Raising the Bar, *Policy Review* (February–March 1996), p 54.

18. Ibid., p. 54.

19. Ibid., p. 56.

20. See, e.g., James Coleman, Thomas Hoffer, and Sally Kilgore, *High School Achievement: Public, Catholic, and Private Schools Compared* (New York: Basic Books, 1982); and Andrew Greeley, *Catholic High Schools and Minority Students* (London: Transaction Books, 1982).

21. Derek Neal, "The Effects of Catholic Secondary Schooling on Educational Achievement," *Journal of Labor Economics*, vol. 15, p. 98.

22. Ibid., p. 100.

23. Stern, "The Invisible Miracle of Catholic Schools," pp. 14–16.

24. Ibid., pp. 16–17.

25. Chubb and Moe, *Politics, Markets & America's Schools* (Washington, D.C.: Brookings Institution, 1990), p. 140.

26. Transcript of Evidentiary Hearing, *Jackson v. Benson*, No. 95-CV-1982 (Dane County, WI, Circuit Court, August 15, 1996), p. 31.

27. Evidentiary Hearing Transcript, p. 40.

28. *Davis v. Grover*, 480 N.W.2d 460, 477 (1992) (Ceci, L., concurring). The battle over school choice in Milwaukee is chronicled superbly in Daniel McGroarty, *Break These Chains: The Battle for School Choice* (Rocklin, Ca.: Prima Publishing, 1996).

29. For an excellent essay on that topic, see Glenn C. Loury, "Getting Involved: An Appeal for Greater Community Participation in the Public Schools," *Washington Post* (August 8, 1995), p. R1.

30. Steven Walters, "Choice Not Siphoning Off MPS' Best Pupils," *Milwaukee Sentinel* (February 8, 1995).

31. Jay P. Green, Paul E. Peterson, and Jiangtao Du, *The Effectiveness of School Choice in Milwaukee: A Secondary Analysis of Data from the Program's Evaluation* (Cambridge, Mass.: Harvard University John F. Kennedy School of Government, 1996).

32. Evidentiary Hearing Transcript, p. 77.

33. Ibid., p. 48.

34. Ibid., p. 51.

35. Ibid., p. 165.

36. Ibid., p. 98.

37. Ibid., p. 102.

38. Ibid., p. 106.

39. Affidavit of Fannie Lewis, *Gatton v. Goff,* Case No. 96CVH-01-193 (Court of Common Pleas of Franklin County, Ohio), pp. 4–5.

40. Affidavit of Jennifer Kinsey, *Gatton v. Goff,* pp. 3–5.

41. His findings will be published in a forthcoming book. Moe shared his preliminary findings at the Institute for Justice Retreat, Alden Ranch, September 28, 1997.

42. Quoted in Nina Shokraii, "Free at Last: Black America Signs Up for School Choice," *Policy Review* (November/December 1996), p. 21.

43. Christopher Broderick, "Rocky Mountain Rift," *The American School Board Journal* (October 1995), p. 32.

44. Robert C. Johnson, "In '96 Sessions, Charter Laws Keep Spreading," *Education Week* (December 4, 1996), p. 14.

45. Center for Education Reform, *Charter School Statistics* (November 1, 1996).

46. Chester E. Finn, Jr. and Diane Ravitch, "Charter Schools—Beware Imitations," *Wall Street Journal* (September 7, 1995).

47. Chester E. Finn, Jr., Bruno V. Manno, and Louann A. Bierlein, "The Empire Strikes Back," *The New Democrat* (November/December 1996), p. 8.

48. Finn and Ravitch, "Charter Schools—Beware Imitations."

49. Mark Buechler, *Charter School Legislation: State Rankings Based on Degree of Expansiveness* (Washington, D.C.: Center for Education Reform, 1996).

50. For a different rating system yielding similar results, see Chester E. Finn, Jr., Bruno V. Manno, and Louann Bierlein, *Charter Schools in Action: What Have We Learned?* (Indianapolis, Ind.: Hudson Institute, 1996).

51. Finn, Manno, and Bierlein, *Charter Schools in Action*, p. 101.

52. Hugh Pearson, "An Urban Push for Self-Reliance," *Wall Street Journal* (February 7, 1996).

53. Finn, Manno, and Bierlein, *Charter Schools in Action*, p. 88.

54. Center for Education Reform, *Charter School Statistics*.

55. Hal Mattern, "Charter Schools Drawing At-Risk Kids," *Arizona Republic* (November 7, 1995).

56. Finn, Manno, and Bierlein, *Charter Schools in Action*, p. 14.

57. Matthew Robinson, "Unshackling Nation's Schools," *Investor's Business Daily* (November 19, 1996), p. A1.

58. Quoted in Finn, Manno, and Bierlein, *Charter Schools in Action*, p. 62.

59. Ibid., p. 91.

60. Ibid., p. 61.

61. Clint Bolick, "Charter Reformer: Arizona's Superintendent of Schools Points the Way to an Education Revolution," *National Review* (April 6, 1998), pp. 42–44.

62. Groups like People for the American Way and the ACLU have different motives than the unions but are equally committed to resisting choice-based education reform. People for the American Way, in particular, views the public schools as a means of molding children in conformity with politically correct values, and accordingly it fears parental choice as a means of subverting those preferred values. Fortunately, the U.S. Supreme Court has repeatedly confirmed the primary role of parents in directing their children's education. See, e.g., *Pierce v. Society of Sisters*, 268 U.S. 510 (1925); *Wisconsin v. Yoder*, 406 U.S. 205 (1972).

63. See Clint Bolick, *The Affirmative Action Fraud: Can We Restore the American Civil Rights Vision?* (Washington: Cato Institute, 1996), pp. 51–68.

64. Nat Hentoff, "A Different Sort of Affirmative Action," *Washington Post* (February 8, 1997), p. A21.

65. Hoffman, "Shifting Gears," p. 33.

66. Hentoff, "A Different Sort of Affirmative Action," p. A21.

67. Kenneth R. Weiss, "UC Chief Seeks to Expand Programs to Aid Minorities," *Los Angeles Times* (January 16, 1998). Early results show as much as a 20 percent improvement in test scores among the students in the program. See Anastasia Hendrix, "Tutoring Boosts Youth Test Scores, UC Study Shows," *San Francisco Examiner* (February 14, 1998).

68. See, e.g., *Florence County School District Four v. Carter*, 510 U.S. 7 (1993).

69. Theodore J. Forstman and Bruce Kovner, "How to Energize Education," *New York Times* (January 3, 1998).

CHAPTER 4: ECONOMIC LIBERTY

1. Taalib-din Abdul Uqdah, "Redefining Bureaucracy," *Liberty & Law* (Institute for Justice newsletter) (Spring 1993), p. 3.

2. John Tierney, "Man with a Van," *New York Times Magazine* (August 10, 1997).

3. Ibid.

4. See, e.g., *Williamson v. Lee Optical*, 348 U.S. 483 (1955); *City of New Orleans v. Dukes*, 427 U.S. 297 (1976); *Federal Communications Commission v. Beach Communications, Inc.*, 508 U.S. 307 (1993).

5. 83 U.S. 36 (1873).

6. See Clint Bolick, *Unfinished Business: A Civil Rights Strategy for America's Third Century* (San Francisco: Pacific Research Institute, 1990), pp. 47–91.

7. The *Slaughter-House Cases* led two decades later to the infamous *Plessy v. Ferguson*, 163 U.S. 537 (1896), and the "separate but equal" era. *Plessy* was set up to test the constitutionality of laws mandating segregated railroad cars. Because *Slaughter-House* drained all content from the privileges or immunities clause, Adolph Plessy did not have available the argument that the law violated his freedom of contract. Instead, he was forced to argue that the 14th Amendment's equal protection clause prohibited segregation—a much more difficult argument from the standpoint of constitutional intent. For a fascinating discussion of *Plessy* and its origins in *Slaughter-House*, see Charles A. Lofgren, *The Plessy Case* (New York: Oxford University Press, 1987).

8. William Julius Wilson, "Dying for a Job," *Phoenix Gazette* (September 2, 1996), p. B5.

9. Andrew Hacker, *Two Nations: Black and White, Separate, Hostile, Unequal* (New York: Charles Scribner's Sons, 1992), p. 103.

10. William Julius Wilson, *When Work Disappears: The World of the New Urban Poor* (New York: Alfred A. Knopf, 1996), p. 31.

11. Wilson, "Dying for a Job."

12. Wilson, *When Work Disappears*, p. 21.

13. Ibid., pp. 52–53.

14. Ibid., p. 22.

15. Ibid., p. 22.

16. Fred Siegel, "Libs to City: Drop Dead," *Policy Review* (September/October 1997), p. 21.

17. William H. Mellor, "No Jobs, No Work," *New York Times* (August 31, 1996).

18. Jason L. Riley, "Return to Self-Reliance," *Wall Street Journal* (August 13, 1997).

19. See Laurie Goodstein, "From Pulpit, Pitches for the Material World," *Washington Post* (December 26, 1996); Courtland Milloy, "A Collective Source of Black Power," *Washington Post* (December 15, 1996), p. B1.

20. Ibid.

21. Ibid.

22. Quoted in Milloy, "A Collective Source of Black Power."

23. Stan Torgerson, "Tribal Chief Influenced by World View," *The Meridian Star* (April 21, 1997). I had the good fortune to visit the Mississippi Choctaw reservation in spring 1997, and can report that the community's economic health is robust, its social infrastructure is solid, and the chief is a remarkable man.

24. Damon Darlin, "Rebellions on the Reservations," *Forbes* (May 19, 1997), pp. 88–99.

25. See "Driving the Poor Out of Business," *Wall Street Journal* (March 3, 1997); Thomas G. Donlan, "Shame of the Cities," *Barron's* (February 17, 1997); Merle English, "Banning Van Ban," *Newsday* (February 11, 1997).

26. Thanks to Max Kadalov for that metaphor. My colleagues Chip Mellor, Nicole Garnett, and Deborah Simpson are prosecuting a federal lawsuit against the ban on

commuter vans. In August 1997, in the face of a media barrage and pressure from Mayor Rudy Giuliani, the New York City Council relented and awarded Vincent Cummins twenty permits for commuter vans—the first significant commuter van business ever authorized in Brooklyn. But the barriers remain in place and exclude other companies, and even authorized vans are severely limited in the scope of permissible operations.

27. See, e.g., Walter Williams, *The State Against Blacks* (New York: McGraw-Hill, 1982).

28. See, e.g., Clint Bolick, *Grassroots Tyranny: The Limits of Federalism* (Washington: Cato Institute, 1992), pp. 141–52; Charles Oliver, "How Cities Keep the Poor Down," *Investor's Business Daily* (September 18, 1996).

29. The cities—New York, Baltimore, Boston, Charlotte, Detroit, San Antonio, and San Diego—were chosen as a representative cross-section of urban America.

30. Dana Berliner, *Running Boston's Bureaucratic Marathon* (Washington: Institute for Justice, 1997), p. 1.

31. Dana Berliner, *How Detroit Drives Out Motor City Entrepreneurs* (Washington, D.C.: Institute for Justice, 1997), p. 3.

32. Ibid., p. 13.

33. William H. Mellor, *Is New York City Killing Entrepreneurship?* (Washington: Institute for Justice, 1996), pp. i and 1.

34. Clint Bolick, *Brightening the Beacon: Removing Barriers to Entrepreneurship in San Diego* (Washington, D.C.: Institute for Justice, 1997), p. 18.

35. See Bolick, *The Affirmative Action Fraud*, pp. 60–61.

36. Walter Williams, *The State Against Blacks* (New York: McGraw-Hill, 1982), p. 123.

37. Interview with Leroy Jones by Sabrina Sandusky, May 13, 1997.

38. A. Webster, E. Weiner, and J. Wells, *The Role of the Taxicab in Urban Transportation* (Washington: U.S. Department of Transportation, 1974). Dollar figures from the 1974 study were converted to 1992 dollars.

39. Kenneth R. Harney, "Senator Seeks to Broaden Tax Rules on Home-Based Business Deductions," *Washington Post* (February 1, 1997), p. F1.

40. Quoted in DeLollis, p. 43.

41. Katherine Shaver, "For 'The Muffin Lady,' Some Home-Baked Troubles," *Washington Post* (February 13, 1997), p. A1.

42. Kathleen Purvis, "Want to Bake Something to Sell? Better Bake It in a Business Zone," *Charlotte Observer* (June 8, 1996), p. 1A. This article describes the plight of Thelma Connell, an elderly woman who was informed by Charlotte zoning officials that home-based businesses that produce goods for sale—even pillows and canned jams—are unlawful.

43. *Brown v. Barry*, 710 F. Supp. 352 (D.D.C. 1989).

44. *Santos v. City of Houston*, 852 F. Supp. 601, 608 (S.D. Tex. 1994).

45. Two of my colleagues deserve enormous credit for this success: my partner Chip Mellor litigated the case; and John Kramer, the Institute's Director of Communications, choreographed the media blitz.

46. Jones interview.

47. See Bolick, *Grassroots Tyranny*, p. 144; see also S. David Young, *The Rule of Experts: Occupational Licensing in America* (Washington: Cato Institute, 1987).

48. Quoted in Barbara DeLollis, "Today's Female Passion for Entrepreneurship," *The American Enterprise* (July/August 1997), p. 43.

49. See George F. Will, "Can't Get the Government Out of Their Hair," *Washington Post* (August 3, 1997).

50. *Cornwell v. California Board of Barbering and Cosmetology*, 962 F. Supp. 1260 (S.D. Cal. 1997).

51. "Braiders Fight for Right to Earn a Living," *University of San Diego School of Law Motions* (February/March 1997), p. 10.

52. Quoted in Nina J. Easton, "Welcome to the Clint Bolick Revolution," *Los Angeles Times Magazine* (April 20, 1997), pp. 30 and 32.

53. Alan Reynolds, "Even in Boom, Minimum Wage Destroys Jobs," *Wall Street Journal* (August 20, 1997).

54. The lawsuit, *Brazier Construction Co. v. Reich*, is pending in federal district court in Washington, D.C. My colleague Dana Berliner and I are the lead attorneys.

55. Most of the quotes in this section are contained in depositions in the lawsuit. This section was published in slightly different form in Clint Bolick, "The Revolt Against the Davis-Bacon Act," *The American Enterprise* (January/February 1997).

56. Quoted in Frank Swoboda, "The Battle That Business Lost," *Washington Post* (February 11, 1996), p. H1.

57. Mellor, *Is New York City Killing Entrepreneurship?*, p. 3.

58. For a discussion of the Local Government Antitrust Act of 1984, which limited antitrust liability of local governments, see Clint Bolick, *Changing Course: Civil Rights at the Crossroads* (New Brunswick, N.J.: Transaction Books, 1988), pp. 133–34.

59. Harney, p. F1.

60. Ronald Brownstein, "Local Activism Shows Way to New Consensus on Reviving Inner City," *Los Angeles Times* (December 22, 1997).

61. Antonin Scalia, "Economic Affairs as Human Affairs," in James A. Dorn and Henry G. Manne, eds., *Economic Liberties and the Judiciary* (Fairfax, Va.: George Mason University Press, 1987), p. 37.

CHAPTER 5: COMMUNITY RENEWAL

1. Quoted in Heather Mac Donald, "Welfare Reform Discoveries," *City Journal* (Winter 1997), pp. 24–25.

2. Quoted in Jason DeParle, "Getting Opal Caples to Work," *New York Times Magazine* (August 24, 1997), p. 33.

3. Charles Murray, *Losing Ground* (New York: Basic Books, 1984).

4. DeParle, "Getting Opal Caples to Work," p. 34.

5. Quoted in John F. Harris and Judith Havemann, "Welfare Rolls Continue Sharp Decline," *Washington Post* (August 13, 1997), p. A1.

6. DeParle, "Getting Opal Caples to Work," p. 61.

7. Gabriel Escobar, "Graduating with Honor from the Streets of D.C.," *Washington Post* (August 24, 1997).

8. Ibid., p. A16.

9. Robert Rector, "Welfare Reform," Stuart Butler and Kim Holmes, eds., *Issues '96: The Candidate's Briefing Book* (Washington, D.C.: 1996), p. 199.

10. Ibid., "Welfare Reform," p. 200.

11. Harris and Havemann, "Welfare Rolls Continue Sharp Decline," p. A1.

12. Rector, "Welfare Reform," 208.

13. Harris and Havemann, "Welfare Rolls Continue Sharp Decline," p. A6.

14. Barbara Vobejda and Judith Havemann, "In Welfare Decisions, One Size No Longer Fits All," *Washington Post* (June 30, 1997), pp. A1 and A8.

15. Hanna Rosin, "About Face," *The New Republic* (August 4, 1997), p. 16.

16. Harris and Havemann, "Welfare Rolls Continue Sharp Decline," p. A1. A review and analysis of the comparative success of states in reducing their welfare rolls is provided in Merrill Matthews and Kirstin A. Becker, *Making Welfare Work: Lessons from the Best and Worst State Welfare Reform Programs* (Dallas, Tex.: National Center for Policy Analysis, 1997).

17. Charles Murray, "What Government Must Do: Make Welfare Unappealing or Reform Will Fail," *The American Enterprise* (January/February 1998), p. 72.

18. Presentation by Douglas Besharov, Institute for Justice Retreat, Alden Ranch, Geyserville, California, September 28, 1997.

19. DeParle, "Getting Opal Caples to Work," p. 33.

20. Tommy Thompson and William J. Bennett, "The Good News About Welfare Reform: Wisconsin's Success Story," *Heritage Lectures* No. 593 (March 6, 1997).

21. See Heather Mac Donald, "Welfare Reform Discoveries," pp. 24–25.

22. See Robert Rector, "Wisconsin's Welfare Miracle," *Policy Review* (March/April 1997), pp. 20–26.

23. Mac Donald, "Welfare Reform Discoveries," pp. 18–21.

24. Ibid., p. 18.

25. "Why Welfare to Work Programs Don't Work Wonders," *Washington Post* (February 23, 1997), p. A19.

26. Wilson, *When Work Disappears*, p. 181.

27. Aaron Steelman, "Welfare to Work: What Happens When Recipient Meets Employer?" *The American Enterprise* (January/February 1998), p. 60.

28. Katherine Boo, "Reaching Up for the Bottom Rung," *Washington Post* (February 23, 1997), p. A18.

29. Kay S. Hymowitz, "At Last, a Job Program That Works," *City Journal* (Winter 1997), pp. 32–39.

30. Rosen, "About Face," pp. 16–19.

31. Dana Milbank, "Under the Underclass," *The New Republic* (August 4, 1997), p. 20.

32. Ibid., p. 21.

33. Ibid., p. 24.

34. Murray, "What Government Must Do," p. 72.

35. Robert Rector, "Washington's Assault on Welfare Reform," *Heritage Foundation Issue Bulletin* No. 244 (August 14, 1997).

36. Marvin H. Olasky, "Welfare Reform: The End of Compassion?" *USA Today Magazine* (March 1997), p. 26.

37. Wade Horn and Andrew Bush, *Fathers, Marriage, and Welfare Reform* (Indianapolis, Ind.: Hudson Institute, 1997), p. 3.

38. John J. DiIulio, Jr., "Bring Back Shotgun Weddings," *The Weekly Standard* (October 21, 1996), p. 15.

39. Douglas J. Besharov and Timothy S. Sullivan, "Welfare Reform and Marriage," *Public Interest* (Fall 1996), pp. 81–94.

40. Quoted in DiIulio, "Bring Back Shotgun Weddings."

41. Besharov and Sullivan, "Welfare Reform and Marriage."

42. DiIulio points to "scattered evidence that welfare time limits may trim illegitimacy rates," and to a National Academy of Sciences study showing that every one percent increase in welfare benefits triggers a 1.2 percent increase in out-of-wedlock births. DiIulio, "Bring Back Shotgun Weddings."

43. Jon Jeter, "Making Family a Man's World," *Washington Post* (July 8, 1997).

44. DiIulio, "Bring Back Shotgun Weddings."

45. Jeter, "Making Family a Man's World," pp. B1 and B8.

46. See William D. Eggers, "There's No Place Like Home," *Policy Review* (May/June 1997), p. 43.

47. Dale Russakoff, "One Child's Chaotic Bounce in Mother Government's Lap," *Washington Post* (January 18, 1998), pp. A1 and A22–23.

48. Sam Skolnik, "Adoption Delayed, Family Denied," *Legal Times* (February 24, 1997), p. 1.

49. Eggers, "There's No Place Like Home," p. 46.

50. Dale Russakoff, "1997 Law Redefines Child-Protection Policies in Place Since 1980," *Washington Post* (January 18, 1998), p. A23.

51. Rita J. Simon, Howard Altstein, and Marygold S. Melli, *The Case for Transracial Adoption* (Washington, D.C.: American University Press, 1994).

52. See Steven A. Holmes, "Bitter Racial Dispute Rages Over Adoption," *New York Times* (April 13, 1995). My colleague Donna Matias and I served as lead counsel in the lawsuit against the Texas Department of Protective and Regulatory Services.

53. See Steve Vogel and Bill Miller, "D.C. Woman Who Killed Daughter is Awarded Custody of Young Son," *Washington Post* (December 31, 1997), p. A1; Tucker Carlson, "Horror in the Court," *Weekly Standard* (January 26, 1998), p. 14. My colleague Donna Matias and I are members of the legal team appealing the custody award.

54. Paul Bonner, "Ex-Gang Member Hits Streets to Help Youths," *Durham Herald-Sun* (January 19, 1997), p. B1.

55. Hillary Rodham Clinton, *It Takes a Village and Other Lessons Children Teach Us* (New York: Touchstone Books, 1992).

56. Robert L. Woodson, Sr., *The Triumphs of Joseph* (New York: Free Press, 1998).

57. Glenn C. Loury and Linda Datcher Loury, "Not by Bread Alone," *The Brookings Review* (Winter 1997), p. 13.

58. John J. DiIulio, Jr., "The Coming of the Super-Preachers," *Weekly Standard* (June 23, 1997), p. 24.

59. John J. DiIulio, Jr., "Fixing Stained-Glass Windows," *Weekly Standard* (November 10, 1997), p. 18.

60. DiIulio, "The Coming of the Super-Preachers," p. 25.

61. Loury and Loury, "Not by Bread Alone," p. 10.

62. Ibid., p. 11.

63. See Amy L. Sherman, "Little Miracles: How Churches Are Responding to Welfare Reform," *The American Enterprise* (January/February 1998), p. 64.

64. Richard Vara, "A Joy to Behold," *Houston Chronicle* (March 16, 1996), Religion Section, p. 1.

65. Barbara von der Heydt, "Tough Medicine for Welfare Moms," *Policy Review* (May/June 1997).

66. I think those concerns will be proven unsubstantiated. The U.S. Supreme Court has upheld public funding of religiously sponsored programs, so long as participation is voluntary and the religious programs are part of a broader array of programs the government is funding. See, e.g. *Rosenberger v. Rector & Visitors of University of Virginia*, 515 U.S. 819 (1995).

67. Ann O'Hanlon, "Cooperation of Church and State," *Washington Post* (October 13, 1997), pp. A1 and A16.

68. Joe Klein, "In God They Trust," *The New Yorker* (June 16, 1997), p. 42.

69. See Richard Wolf, "Law Lets States Increase Churches' Welfare Role," *USA Today* (October 1, 1997), pp. 1A–2A.

70. "Law Lets States Increase Churches' Welfare Role," pp. 1A–2A.

71. Klein, "In God They Trust."

72. Dan Coats, "Faith-Based Drug Treatment," *Indianapolis News* (April 8, 1997), p. A4.

73. Cheryl Wetzstein, "Abuse Program Believes in Ability Without State Aid," *Washington Times* (March 26, 1997), p. A2.

74. Quoted in William Raspberry, "A License? To Save Lives?" *Washington Post* (October 22, 1992), p. A31.

75. Marvin Olasky, "Addicted to Bureaucracy," *Wall Street Journal* (August 15, 1995).

76. Roy Maynard, "Bully Gets a Black Eye," *World* (August 26/September 2, 1995), p. 17.

77. My colleagues Chip Mellor and Nicole Garnett represented Teen Challenge in their successful negotiations with the State of Texas.

78. Coats, "Faith-Based Drug Treatment," p. A4.

79. Sherrye Henry, "They Are All My Children," *Parade* (May 3, 1987).

80. Quoted in William Raspberry, "Holding Kids to a Higher Standard," *Washington Post* (September 14, 1990).

81. See Howard Husock, "Back to Private Housing," *Wall Street Journal* (July 31, 1997); and "Broken Ladder," *Policy Review* (March/April 1997), pp. 46–50.

82. Husock, "Broken Ladder," p. 47.

83. Husock, "Back to Private Housing."

84. Ibid.

85. See Clint Bolick, *Grassroots Tyranny: The Limits of Federalism* (Washington, D.C.: Cato Institute, 1993), pp. 111–121.

86. Stuart M. Butler, "How Privatization Incentives Can Revive Inner-City Housing," *National Forum: Phi Kappa Phi Journal* (March 22, 1990), p. 14.

87. See "Thoughts on Civil Society," *Policy Review* (March/April 1997), p. 63.

88. Olasky, "Welfare Reform: The End of Compassion?"

89. Ibid. Olasky presents his blueprint in *Renewing American Compassion* (Washington, D.C.: Regenery Publishing, Inc., 1997).

90. "The New Mission for Philanthropy," *Policy Review* (September/October 1997), p. 46.

91. "The New Mission for Philanthropy," pp. 49–50.

92. Seth Gitell, "Your United Way Dollars at Work," *The Weekly Standard* (September 22, 1997), p. 27.

93. The Institute for Justice has challenged mandatory community service programs in public high schools. My colleague Scott Bullock leads that litigation effort.

94. "Dan Coats, Senator for Charity," *The Economist* (February 15, 1997), p. 32.

95. Olasky, "Welfare Reform: The End of Compassion?" For a spirited debate among conservatives over the wisdom of charity tax credits, see Peter S. Barwick, Merrill Matthews, Jr., Robert Rector, Grace-Marie Arnett, and Stanley W. Carlson-Thies, "Charity Tax Credits—And Debits," *Policy Review* (January/February 1998), p. 33.

96. Christine L. Olson, "The American Community Renewal Act of 1997," *Heritage Foundation Issue Bulletin* No. 229 (March 19, 1997), p. 17.

97. Robert Pear, "Clinton to Offer a Child Care Plan, White House Says," *New York Times* (December 14, 1997), p. 1.

98. Michael Kelly, "The Child-Care Experiment," *Washington Post* (January 14, 1998), p. A19.

99. Robert Pear, "Republicans Draft Child-Care Legislation That Would Also Help Stay-at-Home Parents," *New York Times* (January 25, 1998), p. 15.

100. In the context of school choice programs, I have prepared an analysis of constitutional principles that are applicable here as well. See Clint Bolick, "School Choice, the Law and the Constitution," *Heritage Foundation Backgrounder* (September 19, 1997).

CHAPTER 6: FREEDOM FROM CRIME

1. Quoted in Nick Kotz, "Changing Lives," *Washingtonian* (February 1998), p. 84. The article provides an extraordinary account of efforts to intervene in the lives of vulnerable inner-city youngsters.

2. Doug Struck, "In D.C.'s Simple City, Complex Rules of Life and Death: Brash 12-Year-Old Overstepped Bounds," *Washington Post* (April 20, 1997), p. A1; and

Bill Miller, "Slain 12-Year-Old's Brother Testifies at Trial," *Washington Post* (November 25, 1997), p. B1.

3. "U.S. Violent Crime Drops 7%," *Sacramento Bee* (June 2, 1997), p. A1.

4. Morgan O. Reynolds, *Crime and Punishment in America: 1997 Update* (Dallas, Tex.: National Center for Policy Analysis, 1997). For an excellent overview of recent lessons in effective law enforcement, see Eugene H. Methvin, "Mugged by Reality," *Policy Review* (July/August 1997), p. 32.

5. John J. DiIulio, Jr., "The Question of Black Crime," *The Public Interest* (September 22, 1994), p. 3.

6. For one sobering yet too-typical report, see Peter Herman, "Five Die Violently in 24 Hours," *Baltimore Sun* (March 7, 1997), p. 4B. One of the victims of violence was five-year-old Kaprice Dollar, who was struck inside her house by a stray bullet. Fortunately, her wound was not fatal.

7. See Clint Bolick, *Changing Course: Civil Rights at the Crossroads* (New Brunswick, N.J.: Transaction, 1988), p. 42.

8. Randall Kennedy, *Race, Crime, and the Law* (New York: Pantheon Books, 1997), p. x.

9. Jim Sleeper, *Liberal Racism* (New York: Viking, 1997), p. 24.

10. *McClesky v. Kemp*, 481 U.S. 279 (1987).

11. Thernstrom and Thernstrom, *America in Black and White*, pp. 268–77, rebut evidence of systemic bias in arrests, prosecutions, and capital punishment.

12. For an account of this experience, see Clint Bolick, *The Affirmative Action Fraud*, pp. 1–3.

13. Thernstrom and Thernstrom, *America in Black and White*, p. 266.

14. Susan Estrich, *Getting Away with Murder: How Politics is Destroying the Criminal Justice System* (Cambridge, Mass.: Harvard University Press, 1998), p. 92.

15. Kennedy, *Race, Crime, and the Law*, p. 29.

16. Ibid., p. 138.

17. Ibid., p. 160.

18. Ibid., pp. 153.

19. Ibid., p. 4.

20. Patricia Cohen, "One Angry Man: Paul Butler Wants Black Jurors to Put Loyalty to Race Above Loyalty to the Law," *Washington Post* (May 30, 1997), p. B1.

21. Kennedy, *Race, Crime, and the Law*, p. 305.

22. Thernstrom and Thernstrom, *America in Black and White*, p. 517.

23. Ibid., 515.

24. Kennedy, *Race, Crime, and the Law*, p. 26.

25. Thernstrom and Thernstrom, p. 265.

26. DiIulio, "The Question of Black Crime."

27. Thernstrom and Thernstrom, *America in Black and White*, p. 264.

28. Ibid., p. 282.

29. Pierre Thomas, "1 in 3 Black Men in Justice System," *Washington Post* (October 5, 1995), p. A1.

30. See, e.g., Patrick F. Fagan and Robert E. Moffit, "Crime," in Stuart Butler and Kim Holmes, eds., *Issues '96: The Candidate's Briefing Book* (Washington, D.C.: 1996), pp. 234–35.

31. DiIulio, "The Question of Black Crime."

32. Ibid.

33. Kennedy, *Race, Crime, and the Law*, p. 311.

34. Kit R. Roane, "Siege of 163d Street: Police Take Over a Drug-Ridden Block to Save It," *New York Times* (September 21, 1997), pp. 41 and 44.

35. Janet Ward, "NYPD View: New Procedures Credited with Crime Drop," *American City and County* (February 1997), p. 28.

36. Fred Siegel, *The Future Once Happened Here: New York, D.C., L.A., and the Fate of America's Big Cities* (New York: Free Press, 1997), p. 195.

37. See, e.g., Blaine Harden, "As U.S. Curbs Car Theft, District's Rate Rises," *Washington Post* (July 21, 1997), p. A1. The article notes that while auto thefts in New York City declined by 59 percent over the past five years, they increased 27 percent in Washington, D.C.

38. Siegel, *The Future Once Happened Here*, p. 193.

39. Ibid., p. 169.

40. Sleeper, *Liberal Racism*, p. 25.

41. Edwin Meese III and Bob Carrico, "Taking Back the Streets: Police Methods That Work," *Policy Review* (Fall 1990), p. 22.

42. Siegal, *The Future Once Happened Here*, p. 192.

43. William D. Eggers and John O'Leary, "The Beat Generation: Community Policing at Its Best," *Policy Review* (Fall 1995), p. 4.

44. Ibid.

45. Meese and Carrico, "Taking Back the Streets."

46. Reuben Greenberg, "Reclaiming Dangerous Neighborhoods," speech published by the Center of the American Experiment (April 1997).

47. Kent E. Walker, "Police Chief Demands Crime-Free Charleston," *Durham Herald-Sun* (April 13, 1997), p. A1.

48. Tucker Carlson, "Bad Cop: How the Left Is Hijacking 'Community Policing,'" *Weekly Standard* (March 17, 1997), p. 21.

49. Ibid.

50. Carlson, "Bad Cop," p. 25.

51. Eggers and O'Leary, "The Beat Generation."

52. DiIulio, "The Question of Black Crime."

53. Kristan Trugman, "Neighborhoods Pay the Price to Feel Secure," *Washington Times* (January 6, 1997), p. C4.

54. Eggers and O'Leary, "The Beat Generation."

55. Carl T. Rowan, Jr., "D.C. Confidential," *New Republic* (January 19, 1998), p. 20.

56. Robert L. Woodson, Sr., "A D.C. Neighborhood's Hard-Won Peace," *Wall Street Journal* (February 21, 1997). For a discussion of this initiative within the broader context of Woodson's mission, see Michael Janofsky, "Old Friends, Once Felons, Regroup to Fight Crime," *New York Times* (March 10, 1997).

57. John J. DiIulio, Jr., "How to Defuse the Youth Crime Bomb," *The Weekly Standard* (March 10, 1997), p. 20.

58. Leef Smith, "Police Force Grows and Changes with the County: 'Urban' Crimes, Violence by Teens Are on the Rise," *Washington Post* (July 6, 1995), p. V1.

59. Quoted in Pierre Thomas, "Arrests Soar for Violent Crime by Juveniles," *Washington Post* (September 5, 1995), p. A1.

60. DiIulio, "The Question of Black Crime."

61. DiIulio, "How to Defuse the Youth Crime Bomb," pp. 22–23. See also *Preventing Crime, Saving Children: Monitoring, Mentoring, & Ministering* (New York: Manhattan Institute, 1997), which is the second report of the Council on Crime in America, co-chaired by Griffin B. Bell and William J. Bennett.

62. See Andrew Peyton Thomas, "Victims' Wrongs," *Weekly Standard* (March 17, 1997), p. 16.

63. Joe Loconte, "Making Criminals Pay," *Policy Review* (January/February 1998), p. 26.

64. *Payne v. Tennessee*, 501 U.S. 808 (1991).

65. Including my Institute for Justice colleague Scott Bullock, who is seriously misguided on this subject.

66. See Skip Thurman, "Victims' Rights Groups Near a Constitutional Showdown," *Christian Science Monitor* (April 28, 1997), p. 1.

67. Thomas, "Victims' Wrongs."

68. "Highs and Lows in the U.S. War on Drugs," *Washington Post* (September 7, 1997), p. C4.

69. Kennedy, *Race, Crime, and the Law*, p. 351.

70. Milton Friedman, "There's No Justice in the War on Drugs," *New York Times* (January 11, 1998), p. 19.

71. David Simon and Edward Burns, "Too Much Is Not Enough," *Washington Post* (September 7, 1997), p. C1.

72. Simon and Burns, "Too Much Is Not Enough," p. C4.

73. Ibid.

74. "Highs and Lows in the U.S. War on Drugs."

75. James Ostrowski, "Thinking About Drug Legalization," *Cato Policy Analysis* No. 121 (May 25, 1989).

76. See Scott G. Bullock, "Filling the Coffers with Civil Forfeitures," *Legal Times* (November 1, 1993); Henry Hyde, *Forfeiting Our Property Rights: Is Your Property Safe from Seizure?* (Washington, D.C.: Cato Institute, 1995); Roger Pilon, "Can American Asset Forfeiture Law be Justified?" *New York Law Review*, vol. 39, p. 311 (1994).

77. Friedman, "There's No Justice in the War on Drugs," p. 19.

78. Christopher S. Wren, "New Voice in Drug Debate Seeks to Lower Volume," *New York Times* (September 1, 1997).

79. Ibid.

80. Quoted in Arianna Huffington, "Bill Bennett, Drugs and Taxes," *Sacramento Bee* (August 29, 1997).

81. Quoted in Eggers and O'Leary, "The Beat Generation."

CHAPTER 7: EMPOWERMENT, POLITICS, AND FREEDOM

1. Martin Luther King, Jr., "An Address Before the National Press Club," in Washington, ed., in James M. Washington, ed., *A Testament of Hope: The Essential Writings and Speeches of Martin Luther King, Jr.* (San Francisco: Harper, 1986), p. 104.

2. Quoted in Robert B. Dishman, ed., *Burke and Paine on Revolution and the Rights of Man* (New York: Charles Scribner's Sons, 1971), pp. 198 n.2 and 200.

3. Quoted in Albert P. Blaustein and Robert L. Zangrando, eds., *Civil Rights and the American Negro* (New York: Trident Press, 1968), p. 291.

4. Fred Siegel, *The Future Once Happened Here: New York, D.C., L.A., and the Fate of America's Big Cities* (New York: Free Press, 1997), p. 211.

5. Quoted in Siegel, *The Future Once Happened Here*, pp. 50–51.

6. Siegel, *The Future Once Happened Here*, p. 51.

7. Ibid., p. 61.

8. A classic example was the battle over the Civil Rights Act of 1991. When President Bush articulated a principled opposition, he successfully transformed the terms of the debate. But when he later inexplicably capitulated, he reaped no political benefit. See Bolick, *The Affirmative Action Fraud*, pp. 111–114.

9. Thatcher's political tactics and legacy are discussed in Clint Bolick, "Thatcher's Revolution: Deregulation and Political Transformation," *Yale Journal on Regulation*, vol. 12, p. 527 (1995).

10. Quoted in Bolick, "Thatcher's Revolution," p. 533.

11. See Madsen Pirie, "Britain's 'New Labor' Is for Real," *Wall Street Journal* (August 22, 1997).

12. William Raspberry, "Out of Ideas," *Washington Post* (September 26, 1997), p. A25.

13. Quoted in Rochelle Watson, "Robert Woodson's Conservative Prescription for Change," *About . . . Time Magazine* (January 31, 1995), p. 16.

14. Elena Neuman, "Color Them Conservative: Beliefs of Blacks Belie Their Politics," *Washington Times* (October 20, 1993), p. A13.

15. Ibid.

16. Quoted in Elena Neuman, "*Emerge* and the Lure of Racism," *Weekly Standard* (March 24, 1997), pp. 25–26.

17. Watson, "Robert Woodson's Conservative Prescription for Change."

18. Thernstrom and Thernstrom, *America in Black and White*, p. 291.

19. Michael F. Frisby, "White House Reworks Troubled Race Initiative as President Heads for a Town Meeting in Ohio," *Wall Street Journal* (December 3, 1997), p. A24.

20. Bolick, *The Affirmative Action Fraud*, p. 115.

21. Paul Gigot, "GOP Confronts Future Without Hispanics: Adios!" *Wall Street Journal* (August 22, 1997).

22. Bolick, *The Affirmative Action Fraud*, pp. 115–16.

23. See, e.g., Clint Bolick, "Blacks and Whites on Common Ground," *Wall Street Journal* (August 5, 1992).

24. Tucker Carlson, "Christie Whitman, Relic of the Eastern GOP," *Weekly Standard* (November 3, 1997), p. 28.

25. Clifford J. Levy, "Giuliani Sees Significance in Minority Voter Support," *New York Times* (November 6, 1997), p. A24.

26. Gigot, "GOP Confronts Future Without Hispanics."

27. Joel Siegel and Frank Lombardi, "Rudy's Sky-High Poll Vault Soars Above Dems, A New Survey Finds," *New York Daily News* (May 8, 1997), p. 5.

28. Levy, "Giuliani Sees Significance in Minority Voter Support," p. A24.

29. William D. Eggers, "Righting City Hall: Fed-Up Urban Voters are Suddenly Turning to Republicans with Fresh Ideas," *National Review* (August 29, 1994), p. 38.

30. Jason DeParle, "Getting Opal Caples to Work," *New York Times Magazine* (August 24, 1997), p. 59. The governor recounts his experiences in Tommy G. Thompson, *Power to the People* (New York: HarperCollins Publishers, 1996).

31. Ellen Silberman, "Can Black Republicans Carve Niche in the GOP?" *Washington Times* (January 16, 1995), p. 13.

32. Governor Tommy Thompson and Dr. William J. Bennett, "The Good News About Welfare Reform: Wisconsin's Success Story," *The Heritage Lectures* No. 593 (March 6, 1997), p. 15.

33. Quoted in "Wall Street Conference Seen Helping Minorities," *Foxnews Wire* (January 10, 1998).

34. Rochelle L. Stanfield, "A Turning Tide on Vouchers," *National Journal* (September 27, 1997), p. 1911.

35. Samuel G. Freedman, "The Education Divide," *Salon Magazine* (September 30, 1997).

36. Ellen Nakashima, "Outside the Party Lines," *Washington Post* (February 1, 1998), p. B1.

37. William D. Eggers, "City Lights: America's Boldest Mayors," *Policy Review* (Summer 1993), p. 67; see also Eggers, "Righting City Hall"; Peter Beinart, "The Pride of the Cities," *The New Republic* (June 30, 1997), p. 16.

38. Jodi Wilgoren, "L.A. Students Get Offer of Private School Vouchers," *Los Angeles Times* (March 17, 1998).

39. Eggers, "City Lights," p. 16.

40. Terry M. Neal, "Ex-Lawmaker Refuses to be Boxed In," *Washington Post* (January 10, 1998), p. A8.

41. Freedman, "The Education Divide."

42. Neal, "Ex-Lawmaker Refuses to be Boxed In," p. A8.

43. David Kuo, "No More Excuses: Now, Conservatives Like Me Need to Do More for the Poor," *Washington Post* (February 9, 1997), p. C1.

44. Michael S. Joyce, writing in *The Weekly Standard* (August 25/September 1, 1997), p. 27.

INDEX

ABOUT ICS

Founded in 1974, the Institute for Contemporary Studies (ICS) is a nonprofit, nonpartisan policy research institute.

To fulfill its mission to promote self-governing and entrepreneurial ways of life, ICS sponsors a variety of programs and publications on key issues including education, entrepreneurship, the environment, leadership, and social policy.

Through its imprint, ICS Press, the Institute publishes innovative and readable books that will further the understanding of these issues among scholars, policy makers, and the wider community of citizens. ICS Press books include the writings of eight Nobel laureates, and have been influential in setting the nation's policy agenda.

ICS programs seek to encourage the entrepreneurial spirit not only in this country, but also around the world. They include the Institute for Self-Governance (ISG) and the International Center for Self-Governance (ICSG).